PENGUIN BOOKS
BBC BOOKS

PENGUIN BOOKS
BBC BOOKS

Published by the Penguin Group and BBC Enterprises Ltd
Penguin Books Ltd, 27 Wrights Lane, London W8 5TZ,
England
Penguin Books USA Inc., 375 Hudson Street, New York,
New York 10014, USA
Penguin Books Australia Ltd, Ringwood, Victoria, Australia
Penguin Books Canada Ltd, 10 Alcorn Avenue, Toronto,
Ontario, Canada M4V 3B2
Penguin Books (NZ) Ltd, 182–190 Wairau Road
Auckland 10, New Zealand

Penguin Books Ltd, Registered Offices: Harmondsworth,
Middlesex, England

First published 1994

1 3 5 7 9 10 8 6 4 2

Printed in England by Clays Ltd, St Ives plc

A proportion of the royalties on this book will be donated to
charity for the relief of victims of violent crime.

PENGUIN BOOKS
BBC BOOKS
CRIMEWATCH UK

Liz Mills is series producer of *Crimewatch UK*. She started her career as a researcher on *That's Life* and later moved to the features department in BBC Norwich. During 1988 she returned to London and worked for television news before transferring to the documentaries department where she worked as a producer on *Taking Liberties* and *Crimewatch File*.

Liz Mills is married and lives in north London.

This book is dedicated to all those Crimewatch UK *viewers who have contributed to the reduction in crime throughout the years.*

CONTENTS

ACKNOWLEDGEMENTS

Throughout the years that *Crimewatch UK* has been on the air hundreds of police officers have become involved with the cases we have featured and the crimes we have solved. I would like to thank them all, but in particular I have singled out those detectives whose endless patience and cooperation proved invaluable in helping me research this book: Detective Superintendent Mick Williams, Detective Superintendent Bob Taylor, Detective Sergeant Tim Grogan, Detective Chief Superintendent Jack Taylor, Detective Inspector David Hitch, Detective Chief Inspector Chris Kemp, Detective Sergeant Frank Anderson, Detective Superintendent Neale Evans, Detective Constable Jeff Norman, Detective Constable Kevin Shapland, Detective Inspector Christopher Allen, Detective Constable John Judges, Detective Superintendent Malcolm Hargreaves and Detective Sergeant Graeme Bull.

It is impossible to name everyone who has helped throughout the years, but I would like to thank all the police forces who continue to give their full support to the programme, and offer guidance whenever necessary. I am particularly thankful to all the victims, their families and friends who have contributed to this book.

I am also indebted to my husband Allen Mills for his continued support and encouragement, to Jane Turnbull who guided me through the initial intricacies of the publishing world, and to Ruki Sidhwa whose assistance in the research was invaluable.

Finally, I would like to thank various members of the *Crimewatch UK* production team for their encouragement, advice and practical help, notably, Helen Phelps, Julie Hughes, Lesley Cons, Clare Ashford, Martin O'Collins, Linda Cleeve and Jane Stimpson. Many thanks to them all.

PHOTO CREDITS

BBC Books would like to thank the following for providing photographs and for permission to reproduce copyright material. While every effort has been made to trace and acknowledge all copyright holders, we would like to apologise should there have been any errors or omissions.

A Murderer's Game: The Press Association.

The Red Connection: Photos of David Wynne Roberts and Festival Hall cutting: Cumbria Constabulary; Photo of Bronwen Nixon: Tom Houghton Photography.

Birkenhead Serial Rapist: Merseyside Police.

Double Supergrass: Metropolitan Police.

A Chapter of Revelations: ©Jonathan Evans/South London Press.

Double Identity: Essex Police.

FOREWORD

by Nick Ross

Crimewatch UK began as an off-shoot of a BBC 2 law series with a run of just three shows. At the time, precious few chief constables were prepared to trust us with their cases because in their eyes television journalists were usually hostile. We ourselves regarded our programme as an experiment in public service broadcasting; we talked of solving a few crimes but had no serious ambition to create a television classic.

Now, a decade later, *Crimewatch UK* still averages eleven million viewers a month. As a direct result of viewers' phone calls nearly 300 people have been convicted, mostly with very serious offences such as murder, rape and armed robbery. It follows that lives have been saved and many serious crimes have been averted as a result of the *Crimewatch UK* series.

With the luxury of hindsight it is easy to understand the programme's success. Most of us tend to feel powerless about crime, but here is an opportunity to do something about it. Television is usually a passive experience – here is a chance to participate. Fictional detective work has always held a fascination, but here is the real thing. *Crimewatch UK* combines the excitement of cops 'n' robbers with the grittiness of real life and personal involvement.

The programmes have also been brilliantly produced, and Liz Mills has been one of the finest series producers of them all. It requires great technical skill to run such a complex live studio-based show and good social skills to win the trust of police, victims, directors and presenters. But above all, it takes fine editorial judgement to under-play events that are often intrinsically frightening or disturbing.

Unfortunately, the very success of *Crimewatch UK* has led to problems. Notably it has spawned imitators which have not always shared *Crimewatch UK*'s rela-tively low-key approach to reconstructions but which tend nonetheless to be described as 'Crimewatch' pro-grammes. The crime-television ecology has changed over the last ten years, which means we need to be more sen-sitive than ever to issues such as unrealistic fear of crime, voyeurism and copycat offending. On the whole, though, *Crimewatch UK* has consistently done well to avoid the pitfalls while retaining the loyalty and trust of the public it serves.

One thing it has *not* always been able to do enough of, is to report back on cases it has featured. Each pro-gramme is, of course, followed late at night by *Crimewatch Update* and occasionally, too, there are full-length *Crimewatch Files* which describe the progress of a case from start to finish. But, in general, feedback to viewers is hampered by pending police action, rules of libel or contempt of court, or simply lack of programme time.

This book is a record of some of *Crimewatch UK*'s successes. It includes details that have not previously been made known. Every case recorded in this book was solved by information from *Crimewatch UK* viewers. It is both a tribute to them and a testament to the fact that crime is not an unstoppable tidal wave, but something which all of us can tackle and help to solve, that this book has been written.

1

A MURDERER'S GAME

The *Crimewatch UK* production office is large, open-plan and modern. It looks out on the traffic jams of Westway, one of the main highways leading out of London. For part of the month, the place seems quiet while directors and researchers are filming on location, but as the programme night draws near, the office becomes crowded. The presenters and production team huddle over their computer screens, tapping in the scripts; researchers are calling up police incident rooms to follow up past cases or check details of the new ones and make arrangements for the appearance of detectives in the studio. The filmed reconstructions are previewed, edited, scripted and sent for dubbing, which is the process of adding the commentary and mixing the soundtracks.

However, on Wednesday 19 February 1992, the day before one programme, there was an added sense of expectation. *Crimewatch UK* had been approached by the Assistant Chief Constable of West Yorkshire police, Tom Cook, and asked to make a special appeal. By now the programme had a proven track record and, with an audience averaging eleven million, it produces results. This more than anything else was what Assistant Chief Constable Tom Cook and his team needed.

The case he had been handling had made headline news for the past few weeks. Stephanie Slater, an estate agent, had been kidnapped and held for ransom. They believed that the same man had killed Julie Dart nearly seven months earlier and, ever since, he had been playing some kind of game with the police, taunting and goading them through countless letters, yet still he was at large and a real danger to the general public. In their bid to catch him, the police had released details to the press before, but tonight, on *Crimewatch UK*, there were new clues and everyone was hoping that someone would be able to piece the jigsaw together and name the man.

The *Crimewatch* appeal focused on four main clues: two artist's impressions of the man himself, the first recalled by Stephanie, the other by a colleague; a description of his car, a small red hatchback; a picture of a railway badge seen on his jacket, by both Stephanie and a neighbour; and, finally, the biggest clue of all, the actual voice of the kidnapper.

At twenty past nine, the *Crimewatch* studio was tense. Police officers were in their seats, waiting for the telephones to start ringing. The floor manager signalled to everyone to be quiet. The rehearsal time had slipped by and the red lights were flashing; it was just two minutes to transmission. Pieter Morpurgo, the studio director in charge of the programme on transmission day, sat in the control room, or gallery as it is sometimes called. This is a small, cramped room, and on either side of him were the vision mixers and production assistants. The production assistants are responsible for counting the programme on and off the air, and the timings have to be precise. Facing him and the team, were twelve monitors. All of them were small television screens except one, a larger one in the centre, and it showed the image that was being transmitted direct to the viewers in their homes.

As the red lights were flashing, Pieter Morpurgo was making a note of last-minute script changes and giving a final reminder to the lighting director to fade up after the opening titles. Everyone was waiting for their cue. The studio floor was now in darkness, and the only sound to be heard was the weatherman on BBC 1 giving tomorrow's forecast. When two little white dots appeared on the top left-hand corner of the screen, visible only to those who know where to look, it meant that there were just thirty seconds to go. The technical staff and director were poised and, when the dots disappeared, he shouted, 'Run VT.' The titles rolled and the programme was now on the air. Nick Ross, one of the presenters, began, 'In a few minutes you'll hear the voice of the man who kidnapped Stephanie Slater. It's the voice of someone who may well have been involved in other major crimes of course, including murder.'

The police were pinning all their hopes on the next forty-five minutes. Millions of people were going to be watching and listening to every detail in the hope that they could help catch an extremely dangerous and evil man.

It was to prove one of the best results that anyone could ever have hoped for and, as the events of this remarkable case unfolded, there was to be little doubt that, but for the courage and bravery of the second victim, Stephanie Slater, the police would have been investigating a double murder.

This is the story of a man who committed one of the most chilling crimes of the century. It began in Leeds, West Yorkshire, in the summer of 1991.

Julie Dart was born in Leeds on 1 March 1973. She was an attractive girl with long, dark brown hair. While she was still at school, she got a part-time job at a local cafe and worked weekends and throughout the school holidays. It was there that she met Dominic. They became engaged when Julie was seventeen, then moved into a flat together.

Their relationship was volatile and lasted for three years before they split up. Julie then moved back home to live with her mother, Lynn. This was towards the end of 1990. Although Julie had worked from time to time, just then she was unemployed. She had been unable to get regular work and was on the dole while she hunted for jobs. Her dream was to join the army, and she was about to go for an interview.

Julie was very sociable and loved to go out dancing with her friends. One evening, in May 1991, she went to a club in Leeds and bumped into Dominic. They started seeing each other again. Julie told Dominic that she had got a job at Leeds General Infirmary, working shifts.

However, the truth was that, unknown to her family and friends she was, in fact, in debt. Julie badly needed to pay off the loan so she had turned to prostitution. There was little doubt that this was a stop gap, intending to last for just a few weeks until she had paid off the money. She was only eighteen and knew of no other way to earn the cash.

Julie told her mother that she had got a job at Haselton Laboratories, a research establishment near Leeds General Infirmary. She didn't say that she was see-ing Dominic again, because previously Julie had hinted that he had been violent towards her and Lynn didn't want her to see him again. So, when she went out for the evening and didn't come home, Julie would say that she was with a girlfriend.

On Tuesday 9 July, Julie and Dominic were together at his sister's house. There had been a family christening and Julie had helped to prepare the food. At around 7.45 p.m. Julie said that she had to go to work. She called Dominic later that evening, around 9 p.m., to say that she would be spending the night at home.

Julie had rung home the afternoon of Tuesday 9 July and explained that she would be working until 11 p.m. She said that she would get a taxi home, and added, 'If you want to go bed you can, but leave the door open.' These were the last words Julie spoke to her mother.

When Julie didn't appear the next day, Lynn Dart wasn't unduly alarmed because she thought she must be at her friend's house. However, when two days had passed and there was still no sign of Julie, she became very worried.

On the morning of Friday 12 July, Dominic received a letter. It was from Julie. This and subsequent letters received during the investigation had numerous spelling and grammatical errors. It began 'Hello Dominic', and continued, 'Help me please I've been kidnapped and I am been held as a personal security until next Monday night. Please go and tell my mum straight away.'

Indeed, Dominic telephoned Lynn straight away. It was just before 9 a.m. when he got through to her office and she rushed over to his house immediately. The letter was postmarked 7 p.m., Huntingdon, 11 July, and there was a direct appeal from Julie for her mother to phone the police.

Not knowing what to do, and wondering whether or not the letter was genuine, Lynn tried to contact Julie at work, but when she got through nobody had heard of a Julie Dart. It was at this point that she decided to contact the police.

She went to Gipton police station, near her home, and reported Julie missing. She told the officer that she thought Julie had been staying with a friend, but when Lynn later contacted the friend she said she had not seen Julie for ages. Lynn recalls, 'The letter didn't make any sense. Who would kidnap Julie, and who'd want her for ransom? I just went everywhere looking for her. At night I'd go round the pubs, handing out photographs of Julie, but nobody had seen her for weeks.'

The police spoke to a number of Julie's friends and soon discovered that she had been seen in the Chapeltown area of Leeds, a 'red light' district. The letter was then sent to the Vice Squad and, although Julie was not known to them, it quickly became apparent that a 'new girl' had recently been seen on the streets.

Coincidentally, that same Friday, 12 July, the police themselves had received a letter. It was addressed to 'Leeds City Police', which was strange because the force had changed its name nearly twenty years previously to West Yorkshire police. The letter was postmarked Huntingdon and, because of its content, it immediately went to the Vice Squad at Chapeltown police station.

It said, 'A young prostitute has been kidnapped from the Chapeltown area last night and will only be released unharmed if the conditions below are met, if they are not met then the hostage will never be seen again also a major city centre store (not necessary in Leeds) will have a fire bomb explode at 5a.m. 17 July.'

The author of the note was demanding a ransom of £140 000 and gave strict instructions as to how the money should be divided up.

Detective Superintendent Bob Taylor was put in charge of the case. He had just been promoted to Superintendent and had begun his new job the day before Julie was kidnapped. He had dealt with two other kidnaps before, both of which had been genuine, so he immediately took the situation very seriously. He recalled, 'The link between the two letters was made at Chapeltown police station, and although Julie wasn't known to the Vice Squad, witnesses had been found who had seen her working in the red light area.'

Fingerprints were taken from the initial letter written to Dominic, and from Julie's house. It was quickly established that the letter had indeed been written by Julie, although much of its content and language seemed to be provided by someone else.

The police decided that they must move quickly and raise the money demanded by the kidnapper. The Regional Crime Squad, whose expertise was in surveillance work, was alerted and provided trained couriers for the job. The operation began. They had to drop the money according to the instructions given.

The letter continued, 'Next Tuesday 16 July a WPC will drive to Birmingham New Street station with the money, and await a phone call at the Mercury phone terminal in the waiting room on platform 9, she must wear a lightish blue skirt with the money in a shoulder bag. She must be there by 6p.m. and await the call at 7p.m., she will then be given the location of the next phone call, (after receiving the call she must drive North out of the city on the A38M Aston Expressway to join the southbound M6, this information is given to avoid her getting lost in the city.) She must have enough petrol for at least 200 miles driving, and a pen and pad may also be carried, but no radio or transmitter.'

The writer of the letter added that the hostage, 'will be well fed and well looked after in a home rented for the purpose, she will be guarded 24hrs a day by a PIR detector connected directly to the mains. Once the monies have been withdrawn you will receive the address of the hostage. BEFORE ENTERING THE HOUSE THE ELECTRICITY MUST BE SWITCHED OFF from outside the house, opening the door or any movements will activate the detector.'

The letter also contained numerous spelling mistakes, grammatical errors, and there appeared to be significant damage to the typeface of the typewriter.

The police decided that they must follow the instructions in order to try to save Julie's life. So, on the specified Tuesday evening, a WPC was in place at the Mercury phone box at Birmingham's New Street station, when the phone rang. She picked it up, but the line went dead. She waited for twenty minutes, and when nothing happened, the operation had to be abandoned.

It was deeply frustrating. The police had done everything the blackmailer had asked, but all they could do now was to wait for him to make the next move.

Meanwhile, enquiries into Julie's background revealed that she was due to collect her social security cheque from the DSS, opposite Millgarth police station, on Thursday 18 July. She had little money, and this was her only regular income. They decided to watch the premises for the day and, if Julie didn't appear, then they would break the story to the papers, expressing grave concern for her safety.

They were desperate for more news about her welfare, and anxious for the kidnapper to make contact. However, the next day, when there had been no sign of Julie, the police began to prepare a press statement. Little did they realize, though, that as they were doing so, nearly ninety miles away in Lincolnshire, a farmer had discovered a body. It had now been a week since the letters had arrived.

The farmer and his son had just started fencing off a field when they saw a bundle lying on the grass. It was wrapped in a white and pink striped sheet, tied up with green rope. The farmer cut the rope and a piece of the sheet. He saw the outline of an arm. He immediately called the police.

The next day, Saturday, Lincolnshire police circulated the information to all forces by telex, giving details about the body the farmer had found in the field. It just so happened that Detective Superintendent Bob Taylor was working that weekend and when he looked through the teleprinter messages, the hairs on the back of his neck stood up. His eyes focused immediately on the words 'female, aged 18–30'. He somehow knew immediately that this was Julie and rang the incident room in Lincolnshire. When he gave them details about the ring Julie was known to be wearing and her chipped front tooth, his worst fears were confirmed. A post mortem had already been done and fingerprints from the body were compared with those of Julie Dart. They matched and, by 5.30 p.m., they had a positive identification.

Julie's body was badly decomposed, especially the

upper half. She had been dumped beside a long-abandoned railway line and her body was carefully removed to Grantham for examination by a pathologist.

Preliminary examinations did not reveal a positive cause of death. The pathologist recalled, 'There were some injuries to the skull. There was one at the back of the skull and there was one above the left ear, and underneath that injury there was a fracture of the skull. Now these injuries were consistent with being caused by an instrument such as a hammer, but they were by no means convincing causes of death.' He gave the earliest possible time of death at some time after 6.30 p.m. on Wednesday 10 July.

Ligature marks were found on both arms and both legs, which had been caused by the rope tied around her body after death. However, a mark on Julie's ankle proved to be very interesting. It looked as though links of some kind, or beads, had been tied tightly round her leg.

The sheet and rope wrapped round the body were examined and they provided two important clues. Forensic evidence taken from the sheet revealed a number of extraneous fibres, in particular yellow wool and brown nylon fibres, which seemed to have come from a mustard-coloured carpet. The rope was an unusual colour, and when examined by a forensic scientist this too contained fibres similar to those found on the sheet, and it is likely that these would have been transferred when the body was being wrapped up. So, if the police could find where this had taken place, then they hoped that they would find a source for the mustard-coloured carpet, thus providing a significant forensic link.

Three days after Julie's body had been found (Monday 22 July), the police received another letter. This time it carried a Leeds postmark and the envelope was marked 're Julie Dart'. As in the other letters, the word headquarters was spelt incorrectly as 'Headquaters'.

It began, 'Words will never be able to express my

regret that Julie Dart had to be killed, but I did warn what would happen if anything went wrong, at the time of this letter there has been no publicity, if you do not find the body within a few days I will contact you as to the location, it will have to be moved today as it appears to be decomposing.

'She was not raped or sexually abused or harmed in any way until she met her end, she was tied up and hit a few blows to the back of the head to render her unconscious and then strangled, she never saw what was to happen, never felt no pain or knew anything about it.'

The letter described precisely how Julie had been killed, yet this had never been released to the press. On a second examination, the pathologist confirmed that Julie had died from compression of the neck (strangulation) and head injuries. There was no doubt now that the writer of the letters was the killer and the police felt sure he could kill again.

The murderer continued in his letter, 'I still require the same monies as before under the same conditions If you want to avoid serious fire damage and any further prostitutes life, to contact me place an ad in the Saturdays "SUN" newspaper personal column and a phone call will be made to the box at Leicester Forest East northbound services....'

The letter went on to give details to the courier about when she answered the phone and it added that the ad in *The Sun* must read, 'Lets try again for Julies sake'. (There were typing errors and grammatical mistakes as before.)

The police realized that they were quickly becoming embroiled in some kind of game. To help them understand the blackmailer, they sought the advice of a clinical psychologist, Paul Britton.

Paul works with criminals in hospitals and prisons and said, 'Based on my initial examination, I felt that they were dealing with a complex man, a very careful planner, who was likely to be in his late forties, early fifties. Educationally he would be at least secondary level, but not degree level. Occupationally he would have a high level of technical knowledge, but his technical skills wouldn't be at quite the same level. It was clear that he was a complex games player, he wanted to be viewed and taken very seriously by the police service. He wanted them to engage him as a high-level adversary.'

Three days after the advertisement in *The Sun*, another letter came. This one was handwritten and entitled 'Re Julie Dart'. It acknowledged seeing the ad, warned that another hostage would be taken and set another date for the handover of the money. It seemed that Paul Britton was right and that the whole operation was turning into some kind of game for the killer. What kind of man was it that could do something like this? The police feared he could turn into a serial killer. He needed to be caught, and quickly.

The letter was postmarked York, 29 July 1991, and it told police to expect a phone message at 8.30 p.m. on Tuesday 30 July at a public phone box at Leicester Forest End service station on the M1.

The police again followed the instructions carefully, but, unfortunately, when the message came through on the telephone, the courier could not understand it because of background music. She remembers, 'I immediately realized that it was a tape recording and, because of the background noise, I just couldn't understand what was being said, and the only word that I could make out was services. I was extremely frustrated and obviously very concerned as well because of the fact that this man had obviously killed once and, because I had not got the instructions, there was every chance that he just might kill again.'

Detective Superintendent Bob Taylor recalls, 'All the time, he was testing us – seeing how we would respond to his demands. He was building up the tension between us, and, in my opinion, there had never been any serious attempt to get the money so far.'

The police had by now alerted all staff at Royal Mail House, the main sorting office in Leeds, to intercept any letters addressed to Leeds City Police. The letters were to be retrieved by a police officer wearing gloves who would slit open the envelope, take out the letter with tweezers, photocopy it, and then send it straight to the laboratory for forensic tests.

The day after the aborted call at Leicester Forest East, another letter was received. This time it was postmarked Coventry. It said, 'No go last night was not free Monday afternoon for make-up to get hostage Monday evening – make-up takes hours. Your WPC should have been able to hear I have tried it on an extension.' The letter went on to say, 'Next week I will definitely free all Monday and Tuesday so will have no problem with hostage or incendiary, Bye, ring Tuesday.'

On Tuesday 6 August, the police waited for the call, but it never came. Instead another letter was received, postmarked Nottingham.

It said, 'Could not make it Tuesday evening due to the fact that there was no suitable hostage in the Huddersfield red light area on Monday evening.' It said that a further call would be made on Wednesday 14 August at 8.15 p.m. and 'this will be the last time you will receive a call at the usual location, should anything go wrong you will not then be given the location of the incendiary device or the location of the prostitutes body'.

As instructed, at 8.15 p.m. a WPC was in place at Leicester Forest East. The phone rang and a male voice spoke: 'I am going to have to tell you where to go because my tape recorder's broken.' He explained that last night he had abducted Sarah Davies from Walkman Gardens, Ipswich. He gave instructions: 'I want you to take the M1 northbound to junction 40, not 39, then take the A638 to Wakefield, go an eighth of a mile and on your right-hand side there's a telephone box by a bus stop.' The courier repeated the instructions. She was told to receive the next call at 9.35 p.m.

The details were relayed to the incident room and it soon transpired that Walkman Gardens in Ipswich did not exist. Could this be another part of his game, exerting as much pressure on the police as possible?

The WPC set off along the motorway. She recalls, 'I was very, very elated. We were actually getting somewhere. This man had made contact and we were so very close to capturing him. We'd had all the previous frustrations of no phone calls and not being able to understand messages, and at this point I really felt sure we were going to capture him'.

As planned, the call came through. The man was brief, saying, 'Hello, it's me again. Problems, I'll have to ring you back in half an hour.' The WPC waited and, just after 10.30 p.m., the phone rang. She picked it up, but it kept ringing. Realizing that the cradle had jammed, she hit it with her fist, but it was too late. He never rang back.

The police were very disappointed. Detective Superintendent Bob Taylor recalls, 'When we felt there was a real opportunity to arrest him, our hopes rose, and when nothing came out of it, we were disconsolate. But, after a period of time, we steeled ourselves to this and I think that did more for us than anything else. We were determined to work even harder to get him.'

The police never traced a Sarah Davies. They spent weeks looking at all the Sarahs in Ipswich, trying to find someone who had gone missing. The red light district in Ipswich is Portman Road and detectives interviewed a number of prostitutes to try to find out if there was such a person. However, it seemed that her name was an invention on the part of the kidnapper, as a way of trying to increase the pressure on the police.

The day after the phone call, they had another lead. A workman was collecting debris on the southbound carriageway of the M1, near the Barnsley turning at junction 37, when he saw a white-painted brick with an envelope attached and a cylindrical-shaped plastic container, coloured grey and silver, with two small red lights on the top. He was immediately suspicious and called the police. The device was found underneath the bridge that carries the Dove Valley Trail.

It turned out to be a completely harmless home-made device, but was blown up just to make sure. The debris and the brick were taken away for further examination and South Yorkshire Police circulated the details to all forces.

Detective Superintendent Bob Taylor recalls, 'It soon became obvious that this was our man, and when we visited the scene we realized that this was where he was going to get the money. His plan was quite simple. If the courier on the M1 had been able to hear the voice on the telephone, it would have told her to look for a message underneath the telephone directory shelf. This message would have directed her on to the A628 to another phone box in front of a restaurant. There she would have found another message stuck to the shelf directing her back on to the M1 to go to the bridge at junction 37 where she would have found the brick with the device. The message on the brick told her to place the device on the dashboard of the car and drive to the second bridge. The man was going to stand on top of the bridge and lower a dog lead for the WPC to attach the bundle of money to. He was then going to haul the money up and make good his escape from the lane at the top of the embankment. In the very first letter, the kidnapper had drawn a picture of a bundle with a loop attached, and mentioned attaching a dog lead.'

On 20 August, the police received another letter. It was postmarked Grantham and dated 19 August, 1.15

p.m. It said, 'Game is now ababdoned. You will have to file your papers until I try again, which is what this was all about, as you know I never picked anyone up in Ipswich or planted a devise, I didnt need to following Julies death, you would co-operate with anythink I wanted.' The letter went on to explain why Julie's body was so badly decomposed: 'It was kept in a wheely bin in a greenhouse for two very hot days. I thought this was the best way to keep the body.'

The police now had a number of clues to work from. The white brick found on the motorway was extremely unusual in that the dimensions did not conform to normal brick sizes. It had come from a quarry in Newcastle-under-Lyme and was very rare.

The suspect device that was found with the brick had also been examined by forensic scientists in Wetherby. It was made of plastic, but had been coated with an unusual silver paint. A police officer who kept tropical fish recognized the top and metal rim as having come from a fish food container. When these were compared with a complete fish food container they were identical.

The other clues, apart from the forensic leads, came from the letters themselves. They had been posted from Yorkshire and around the Midlands, so the sender obviously had time to travel, and several words were consistently misspelled. The handwritten letters looked odd and appeared to have been disguised. These were sent to an expert who believed that if the police found the person they thought was responsible for writing them, then he could identify him from his handwriting.

It was now the end of August 1991, and Detective Superintendent Bob Taylor recalls, 'Although the letters as they came in one after another created pressure for us, we knew he was still out there. And while he was there we knew we'd got a chance, and our hopes rose. At this stage the whole team were living, eating and sleeping the inquiry – everybody was regularly working upwards of a twelve-hour day. This case was something different. This fellow was a one-off, and I never doubted that we'd catch him because I didn't think he could walk away from it. There was a fantastic buzz when a letter came in. I was able to read it out to the team because there were no leaks, everyone appreciated the need for secrecy.'

The police were desperate, however, for as much publicity as possible, and in mid August they approached *Crimewatch UK* and asked for a nationwide appeal. The time had come to pull everything together in a bid to flush out the killer.

A full reconstruction was broadcast on 12 September, going over the last few days of Julie's life, describing the clothes she was wearing, and appealing for anyone who had seen her to come forward.

Detective Superintendent Bob Taylor went through details of the letters written by her killer, showing the various postmarks. He described the flaws in the typeface, suggesting that they had been written on a manual typewriter and appealed for anyone who had seen one recently to check whether the flaws matched. He asked for anyone who might have known where Julie had been kept during the time she went missing, and the time her body was discovered, to come forward. The pathologist thought that she had been dead between six and ten days before her body had been dumped, and that it was in the farmer's field for no more than twenty-four hours.

Finally, details of what the killer himself might be like were revealed to the public for the first time. The offender profile built up by clinical psychologist Paul Britton was based on eight points:

- dislike of the police
- older man
- self-taught

- had technical knowledge with reference to PIR (passive infra-red) detectors
- not in a senior position
- probably not killed before
- working alone
- his aim was probably not the murder of Julie Dart, but to obtain £140 000.

The appeal was very emotional and a number of people rang. The police knew Julie had phoned Dominic about 9 p.m. on 9 July, but they had never found out where she made the call from. As a result of the programme, a prostitute rang to say that she had been with Julie that night in a pub called the White Swan, and that this was where she had made the call. Also, two more prostitutes were traced and the police discovered that Julie had been with them in the red light area that night. She had eaten a kebab with one of the girls and then gone off on her own. This was the last time anyone had seen her and the timing seems to suggest that Julie was picked up by her killer around 11.30 p.m.

Just over a month later, on Thursday 17 October, the police received another letter. It was addressed to 'Millgate Police Station', instead of Millgarth, and hand-written. The postmark was Huddersfield and it began, 'As you are no where near on my tail the time has come to collect my £140 000 from you. I do not get any bigger sentence for 2 murders and prostitutes are easy to pick up but as this time you know I mean business I don't need to pick one up until Monday and I have purfected the pick up. The money to be the same as before. On Wed 21 Oct the same WPC will be at the phone box on platform 3 of Carlisle station (bottom of ramp) at 8pm for message (recorded) at 9.15pm approx. I believe you will deliver the money as you will not risk the life of WPC or prostitute.'

In fact, the 21 October was a Monday so, in view of this error, arrangements were made for the courier to be in place on *both* days. However, at the same time and quite unbeknown to the Julie Dart inquiry, a similar threatening letter was sent to British Rail. It had two postmarks: Stoke-on-Trent, and Blackheath. The police have never been able to account for the extra mark. The letter said, 'Unless we receive a cash payment of £200,000, we shall cause the derailment of an express train.' It said that on Wednesday 21 October, two female employees of BR had to be at Crewe station at 3 p.m. One was to wait in the car while the other went to platform 3 and waited for a call at 7 p.m.

The Regional Crime Squad working on the Dart inquiry, through the course of their enquiries, spoke to the Metropolitan police and discovered that they had a railway threat inquiry. The ransom dates coincided with those specified by the Julie Dart murderer and, as a result, a West Yorkshire detective helped compare the letters. He noticed a number of similarities: the writer made use of a stencil and the stencilling was underlined, as in the Dart inquiry. There was a request for the money to be packaged in a similar fashion to that in the Dart inquiry, but, more importantly, a WPC had been instructed to go to a telephone kiosk on a railway station platform as the first point of contact. The envelope used was found to have the same printing error and sticky gum as the one received by the West Yorkshire police earlier.

The Metropolitan police decided that it would not be to their advantage to run the operation in respect of British Rail on the same day that the killer was making a ransom demand against the Julie Dart inquiry's team. Both would have involved extremely large surveillance teams working very close together with all the inherent dangers. So, the police decided not to refuse payment, but to defer the operation.

Meanwhile, the police operation at Carlisle went as instructed in the letter. On the Monday, nothing happened and on the Wednesday nothing happened.

Subsequently, another letter was written to British Rail, postmarked Nottingham, 28 October. It stated, 'Congratulations, you have now qualified for retribution. Within a week or so a small penalty will be imposed in the form of the removal of an electric local pantagraph, and with a little luck the downing of a section of line, a suitable place has not yet been located.'

Nearly a week later, a broken concrete block, a piece of sandstone and some rope were found on a piece of railway track near Millmeece in Staffordshire. Detective Superintendent Bob Taylor recalls, 'Although there were no reports of any damage to trains, what he'd done was incredibly dangerous and could have caused severe damage to the train or train driver. We were left thinking what on earth is this man going to do next.'

As a result of this, Detective Superintendent Bob Taylor was put in charge of the British Rail blackmail inquiry as well as that into Julie Dart's murder. However, he was quite unprepared for the next turn of events.

On Wednesday 8 January, a man calling himself Mr Southall visited Shipways estate agents in Birmingham to collect property details. He was served by a female member of staff and, a week later, he sent a letter requesting details of a property at 153 Turnberry Road. The letter was passed to Stephanie Slater and an appointment made for 10.30 a.m. on Wednesday 22 January 1992.

In early December 1991, Stephanie had applied for a job as a senior negotiator at Shipways estate agents, Great Barr. She was interviewed by the manager, Kevin Watts, and duly appointed to start work on Monday 16 December.

Stephanie Slater was born in Birmingham on 9 November 1966. She lived with her parents and, for most of the time since leaving school in 1984, she had worked for estate agents in the West Midlands area.

That Wednesday morning, Stephanie arrived for work as usual and, at 10.30 a.m. left for her appointment at Turnberry Road. She was a little late, so she parked half on the pavement on double yellow lines. She saw a man waiting outside the house and shouted, 'Mr Southall?' and he replied, 'Yes.' She said, 'Sorry I'm late,' and rushed to open the front door of the house. As she walked past him she thought he looked anxious. He was wearing thick black glasses and had a badge with a train on it pinned to his jacket. They went into the hall-way and living room. Mr Southall appeared to be look-ing down at some papers he was carrying and Stephanie thought that he was not really interested in the property. She invited him to look upstairs. He went into the bath-room and she went into the bedroom. He asked if the house had ever been rented out and Stephanie remem-bers, 'I certainly got the impression that Mr Southall was not interested in this particular property, but I simply put that down to the fact that it was in need of some repair. At this stage I was not afraid of the client.'

Then, as she was about to make her way downstairs, he went back into the bathroom. She heard him call, 'What's that up there?' and, as she went inside, she saw him pointing towards the right-hand corner of the bath-room ceiling, above the bath. 'I walked over to the bath, whilst he stood on the threshold of the doorway. I had my back towards him and I saw what I believed to be a flannel holder. At this stage, Mr Southall suddenly said in a much deeper and harsher voice "All right". I turned round and saw he had both hands raised and extended in front of him towards me, in a threatening manner. I saw that he had a knife in his left hand and what I believed to be a chisel or file in his right hand. It was at this time that I noticed he was wearing gloves.'

Stephanie looked straight at him and her automatic reaction was to grab the weapons: 'I was still wearing my gloves and I grabbed the knife with my right hand

and the chisel with my left. I was absolutely petrified and began screaming. I thought he was going to kill me.' A struggle followed and Stephanie ended up in the bath. She pleaded with him not to kill her. He replied, 'No one's going to kill you. You're not going to be harmed. Where's your car keys?' He then tied Stephanie up, and took her car keys from her coat pocket.

Blindfolded, she was forced out of the house, down the garden path and into the garage. Here she was told to lay back in the front passenger seat, which was reclined, while he got into the driver's seat. He then covered her with a blanket and jacket, and then put a scarf over her face and a gag in her mouth. She thought she was going to be raped, then killed. He secured her seat belt and placed a heavy tool-box on her lap saying, 'This won't be on your lap for very long. It's just to keep you down.'

The time was now 11 a.m. He started the engine and the radio came on automatically to Radio 2. The car smelt of oil, petrol and damp rags. It felt like a painter and decorator's car. They drove for about half an hour, and Stephanie recalls the man shouting, 'We're stopping at traffic lights. Be quiet.' She remembers, 'I lay completely still, too frightened to make a move or sound. I recall hearing the sound of passing traffic and people.'

They drove for about another ten minutes before the car stopped and the man turned to her and said, 'You probably know you've been kidnapped. Everything will be all right if you don't cause any trouble. You'll not die if you don't cause any trouble. Do you understand?' She nodded. He then went on, 'We're going to make a tape to your boss. What's your name?' She replied, 'Stephanie Slater.'

The man then leaned across her and took the jacket, blanket and scarf off her face. The blindfold remained in place, but he took the gag out of her mouth. He got out a tape recorder and had some difficulty in making it work. At the third attempt, Stephanie began to repeat the message: 'This is Stephanie Slater. The time is now 11.45. I can assure you I'm OK and unharmed. Providing these instructions are carried out, I will be released on Friday 31st January. By Wednesday you will need an Ordnance Survey map 103 for Blackburn and Burnley. Kevin Watts must be the person to act as courier and use his car. Next Wednesday, at every point where instructions are given, the boot of the car must be opened for at least thirty seconds. Money must not be marked in any way whatsoever or contain any device whatsoever.'

Once the message was recorded, the man got out of the car to telephone Shipways, and post the tape, along with a letter he had written. He made Stephanie lick the envelope, and then placed the gag back in her mouth and re-tied the scarf, also round her mouth.

Back at Shipways, when the call came through, Sylvia, one of the employees, answered it. A man was asking to speak to Kevin Watts, but Sylvia explained that he was out at the moment. Then the man's voice changed and he said, 'Stephanie Slater – she's been kidnapped. There will be a ransom note in the post tomorrow. Contact the police or anybody and she'll die.' He then hung up.

Sylvia contacted Kevin straight away and he, together with a colleague, immediately went round to the house in Turnberry Road where Stephanie had booked her last appointment. Her car was still outside, parked on yellow lines, and Kevin, sensing that something was wrong, went round to the back of the house. He got in through the French windows and saw the keys to the house on the floor. When he returned to the office, he telephoned the police. He explained the situation and said that someone had just phoned up demanding money and threatening to kill an employee if they did not cooperate. He said the missing girl was Stephanie Slater.

Initially, uniformed officers were sent to the scene,

and a little blood was found in the bathroom and on the door keys. Quickly realizing that a life might be in danger, the house was sealed off and plain clothes detectives were sent to replace the uniformed officers. Once the seriousness of the situation was ascertained, Detective Superintendent Mick Williams was brought in to head the investigation team. He recalls, 'Thankfully, kidnaps are extremely rare. I've only known three in twenty-eight years in the police force. We get lots and lots of different hoaxes in relation to this sort of offence and at the beginning of this inquiry uniformed officers were sent to the scene, and that was definitely a mistake. We recognized that very, very quickly, withdrew the officers from the scene and replaced them with covert officers, so that we wouldn't prejudice Stephanie's life or the inquiry in general.' Immediately, a news blackout was effected because, for as long as Stephanie was held hostage, her life was in danger and so the press were asked to hold all details.

A special tape recorder was set up to monitor incoming calls to Shipways estate agents and, at around 3 p.m., the next call came through and it convinced everyone that this kidnap was no hoax. The message was simple, 'Stephanie's dropped her keys in the hall, so go and lock it up.' This is indeed what had happened. When Kevin Watts had entered the house earlier that day, he had found the keys on the floor in the hall. Why, though, was the kidnapper so keen to ensure that the house was locked up? Was it just another part of his game plan?

The final part of Stephanie's journey that day began somewhere around 4 p.m. A Beach Boys tape was playing in the car; it sounded like their greatest hits. She recalls, 'We travelled at around 50 m.p.h. for at least an hour before I was aware of the car making a slight left turn off the road on to a dirt track. It stopped and I was disorientated. He then said, "No screaming. Not that anybody's gonna hear you out here." He got out and I heard the sound of keys rattling, and a heavy metal door being pulled open a little. I could hear a scraping sound, as if metal was being pulled against metal. The floor surface changed from loose dirt to stone. I was absolutely petrified and felt that I would surely die inside that building. I walked for about forty feet before being sat on a hard wooden chair. Then he said, "We're gonna have to change your clothes. I've got some others here for you to wear." He then gave me a woollen, round necked, sleeveless jumper, a thinner, cotton cardigan and a pair of denim jeans. He put a pair of socks on my feet which reminded me of my Dad's, and he gave me back my boots. He put a sock on each of my hands, telling me that these were to protect my hands from the pressure of the handcuffs. These clothes all felt old and worn.'

Stephanie was then handcuffed both at the wrists and ankles. Her kidnapper asked her if she liked fish and chips, adding, 'Tomorrow night I'll cook you a proper meal.' He went out for about ten minutes and returned with chips, still in the shop paper. She ate only a few. Afterwards he said, 'I'm going to put you in a box within a box and that will be where you sleep. I hope you're not claustrophobic.' Stephanie recalled the man saying, 'Right. You're going to bed' and he led her back towards the mattress.

The man had created a special box for Stephanie to sleep in. It was a wheely bin sawn off at the bottom and he had extended it out with a wooden box that he had made. The only problem was that although he had tested it out himself, he had not catered for the fact that women have larger hips than men and so Stephanie could not get into the lower half of the box without a great struggle: 'He told me to lie on my back and shuffle into a hole in front of me, as if I was getting into a sleeping bag. At this stage I had absolutely no idea what I was shuffling into. I can only describe it as a wooden coffin. My hips got stuck and I said I couldn't get down any more. He replied that I should be able to. I shuffled further at an angle, so my hips could fit. This meant that I was not lying straight. I lay on one hip, with the other pointing up and my knees slightly bent. When my body was inside he took hold of my wrists by the handcuff chain and tied it above my head to what I believe was a metal bar. My elbows were now extended outside the coffin and my hands crossed directly in front of my face. The man said, "Don't pull on the bar because there are boulders above you. If you pull on the bar you'll pull them down and crush yourself. No shouting and no screaming. When I open this door in the morning I want to see the gag and blindfold still on you."'

Just before locking her in the coffin he remarked to Stephanie how calm she was. She remembered saying to him, 'I'm the sort of person who deals with situations calmly. It's not in my nature to scream and shout.' In fact she was petrified, but she had already decided to try to create a rapport with her kidnapper. She remembered, 'I think by acting the way I did, he was able to trust me, and I felt this would be the only way of saving myself.'

Throughout that first night, Stephanie had no idea what kind of a box she was in. She felt certain he would kill her, but she was in so much pain tied up in the box that she felt she was going to die there and then. It was an extremely cold night and she was frozen. She saw angels and the face of Christ. At one point, she thought she was dead.

There had now been two calls from Stephanie's kidnapper to Shipways estate agents and a police briefing was quickly arranged between senior police officers, and Assistant Chief Constable Phil Thomas of the West Midlands Police led the meeting: 'It appears the kidnapper is prepared to negotiate. We can therefore only presume that Stephanie, at this time, is alive and well. Her employers are working with us one hundred per cent, and have agreed to put up the ransom money. The press have been informed and have agreed not to publish anything until Stephanie is found safe and well. It is vital that we do not alert the kidnapper that we are involved. I must re-emphasize to you that Stephanie's life may depend on this.'

When the police visited Stephanie's parents to break the news, they could not believe it. Her mother, Betty, was at home and her father, Warren, was called back from work. He remembers, 'It didn't register at first; it just doesn't happen to normal people. I class myself a working-class person, you always think kidnapping or abduction is linked to business people or film stars. And when they asked for money, we said the only thing we can offer you is the house.'

Meanwhile, because the kidnapper had warned that there would be instructions in the post, detectives got rare consent to intercept the mail for Shipways. The tape was found in the early hours of Thursday 23 January and, later that day, it was played to Stephanie's parents, who confirmed that the voice was indeed that of their daughter.

Almost from the beginning, detectives were looking at possible links with other similar cases and the Assistant Chief Constable of the West Midlands, Phil Thomas, immediately began to talk to his West Yorkshire counterpart, Tom Cook. Assistant Chief Constable Phil Thomas recalls, 'From the very early stages we recognized there may be a link with the Julie Dart murder and, therefore, were not only dealing with a kidnapper, but a kidnapping by a man who had already killed previously.'

Detective Superintendent Bob Taylor was away on a course when information about the Stephanie Slater kidnap came through. He returned on Friday afternoon and went straight to the incident room in Leeds. He looked at the details that had emerged: a neighbour had seen the man standing on the pavement waiting for Stephanie; she recalled that he wore a railway badge on his jacket and looked away when he thought he had been seen. Someone else had seen a red Metro revving up outside the house; this type and colour of car had been seen in connection with Julie Dart. The witness recalled that the man was in his fifties and around five feet two inches. It seemed more and more likely that the kidnapper was the same man who had murdered Julie Dart.

The letter that the police had received with the tape contained a number of similarities to those already received. Spelling mistakes were repeated, along with phrases like 'with a little luck' and, once again, the writer had requested money to be made up in specific bundles.

The first step was to check quietly with dog-handlers in plain clothes that Stephanie had not been murdered and left in Great Barr where she had been kidnapped. At the same time, the police started discreet house-to-house enquiries. They had no idea where the kidnapper was hiding; he could even have been in Turnberry Road in one of the adjacent houses. They had to be very careful because if he had been there and seen or heard anything, he might have taken retribution.

Meanwhile, detectives began doing as much background work as possible, but the secrecy of the inquiry hampered them. There were upwards of a hundred detectives drafted on to the team, but they were very much in the hands of the kidnapper, just waiting for him to make his next move.

A call came through to Warren Slater. It was Sunday 26 January at 2.11 p.m.

'*Is that Mr Slater?*'
'*It is.*'
'*Just listen.*'
'*Hello, Stephanie here. They've allowed me to make a message to you, just to let you know that I'm all right. I'm unharmed. I happened to see West Bromwich Albion lost yesterday to Swansea three two. I want you to know*

I love you, and not to worry too much, and whatever the outcome I'll always love you. Look after the cat for me.'

The family and police now knew that Stephanie was still alive. This was the second time they had heard their daughter's voice since the kidnapping five days earlier. The football match was yesterday, as Stephanie had explained in the tape recording, which meant she was still alive today. They were delighted. It was a real tonic for the family.

Now the police felt that they had no option but to prepare a ransom and, as agreed, it would come from Stephanie's employers. However, the biggest dilemma now was whether or not they should also accede to the kidnapper's demand that her boss, Kevin Watts, should be the courier.

Kevin Watts knew that he had been named as the courier. He was thirty-four and married with three young children. He had been an estate agent all his working life. The police explained to him that his proposed role was a dangerous one. The kidnapper might kill Stephanie and his life would also be in jeopardy. However, Kevin was adamant that he should do the job: 'They simply asked me whether I would be willing to be the courier, and I said yes – anything to ensure the safe release of Stephanie. They spent an awful lot of time with me, coaching me, putting me in the right mental frame of mind to cope with the stresses and strains that I would endure during the evening.'

The police were concerned both for the safety of Kevin Watts and about his ability to respond appropriately in a crisis situation. Past experience has shown that even police officers placed under such pressure have failed to come through. However, on the evidence available, the kidnapper had visited Shipways and it was likely that he had seen Kevin, so they had little alternative than to let him be the courier.

Everyone was now gearing up to Wednesday 29 January – the day the kidnapper had demanded that the ransom be paid in his previous letter. He said his next call would be at 4 p.m. that afternoon.

In fact, the kidnapper rang a day earlier than the police had expected to check that everything was going to plan. He even said that he would get Stephanie to make another tape recording to prove she was alive. This call took the team somewhat by surprise, but Kevin Watts handled the situation extremely well, and it was as a result of this that detectives felt sure he could cope with delivering the money.

Six police teams were on duty on the night. The Regional Crime Squad was responsible for looking after Kevin Watts and the money, and they had to be prepared to travel anywhere in the country. Another team was responsible for looking after Stephanie if she was found, and a third was to take responsibility for her abductor if he was arrested. Then there was the Holmes team and the Intelligence Squad. The operation was run by Detective Chief Superintendent Mick Foster, who led the briefing: 'We have a plan involving up to a thousand police officers. We'll use number one and number three Regional Crime Squads as well as our own. As you know, he's pointed us in the direction of Blackburn and Burnley, but we know he's got links with Yorkshire and Lincolnshire. Kevin Watts will have a microphone, and we'll keep him under surveillance wherever he travels'.

The police had two alternatives as to when they should arrest their man. The first was as Kevin dropped off the money, while the second, more risky, option was to keep him under surveillance after the drop, in the hope that they could recover the money, then arrest the kidnapper and release Stephanie. Such was the risk to Stephanie's life, that detectives decided they would try to arrest him at the drop.

Stephanie had spent her last night in captivity sleeping on a mattress, next to her kidnapper. From the beginning he had promised her that on the final night she would not have to sleep in her coffin. When she awoke on Wednesday morning, she recalled, 'He told me to put the blindfold on almost immediately. He informed me that I had slept restlessly throughout the night. He gave me my usual porridge and told me he was busy and had lots of phone calls to make. He then returned me to my box. It was about 9.15 a.m. The man then went out, leaving me in my box, and he came back around 12 midday. He told me that he would be busy, but that he would be back between 8 and 9 p.m. as he was expecting a call from his mate at 9 p.m. He said, "Then you'll be free."'

When Kevin Watts left home that morning, he waved to his family and wrote the letters in the air 'I love you'. He recalls, 'It never crossed my mind that I wouldn't see my wife again. I had every confidence that the police on the evening, as well as myself, would make sure that I returned safely.'

That afternoon, at 3.23 p.m., the phone rang at Shipways. A man's voice said:

'Hello, Kevin Watts?'
'Speaking.'
'Have you got it?'
'Yes, I have.'
'Go to Glossop station.'
'Glossop, could you spell that please?'
'G L O S S O P, west of Manchester. There's a telephone box inside the entrance hall. Only one. And you'll get a further message at 7 o'clock.'
'7 p.m.?'
'Yes. If anything goes wrong and you don't make it there, I want you there as soon as you can. If anything goes wrong, you ring your office up. It's an hour and a half's journey and it's sunny. I'm in Glossop now and it's sunny here.'

The caller explained that Stephanie was OK and that she would be released tomorrow night, just after 12 o'clock. A short recorded message was then played from Stephanie: 'My parents' names are Betty and Warren Slater. I am frightened, but unharmed.'

Kevin was now ready to begin his long and arduous journey. The weather had been horrific – dense, freezing fog – and the drop was going to be in the dark. His car was fitted with a two-way radio, and he had in his possession a transmitter. The microphone would relay his voice back to headquarters, so it was important that he repeated every instruction as and when he got it. This would enable the controller at headquarters to pass the information to the surveillance team.

Wearing a bulletproof vest, he set off up the M6 towards Manchester. The police teams were all on standby, ready to go at a minute's notice. Detective Superintendent Mick Williams recalls, 'The atmosphere was absolutely electric. We were all hoping and praying that everything would go according to plan.'

Kevin pulled into Glossop station and, when he got out of his car, a woman approached him saying that her indicators had broken down and she did not know what to do. He remembered, 'I'd been told that I may be approached by people by way of a test, so at that time in view of the fact that it was such an unusual type of conversation, something you wouldn't come across at all in a normal day, I thought that quite possibly she was mixed up with this, and it threw me completely.'

Kevin approached the telephone kiosk, looked around and saw several people staring in his direction. It was difficult to know who, if anyone, was involved. Then, the telephone began to ring. It made him jump. He picked it up, 'Kevin Watts,' he said and the caller said, 'Leave the station, go right, go down to the crossroads, you'll see a telephone box, inside you'll find a message underneath the parcel shelf which will contain instructions.'

Kevin walked out of the train station towards the telephone box, which was about 200 yards further down the road. He was looking around all the time, observing the people as they walked by. When he got to the phone box, he fumbled about, looking for the note. Eventually he found it and read it out aloud: 'It says: Take B6105 (which is the road outside the station), uphill, and continue until joining A628".' He then read it to himself several times, trying to remember the instructions.

Back at the control room, Detective Chief Superintendent Mick Foster was briefing detectives with a map: 'He's been sent over the top of the Pennines to Yorkshire, just south west of Barnsley. There he's to turn right on to the A629 where he'll find another message in a telephone box about one and a half miles down the road.'

Kevin was told that he had to be at the next phone box by 7.40 p.m. If he missed the time, then there would be a message waiting for him. He was told to enter the box at the allotted time, and at some time or other he would be observed.

It was now 7.30 p.m. and, as Kevin got into his car, he knew that he was not going to make it on time. He took several deep breaths, collected his thoughts and tried to keep calm. He hoped that the next message would be waiting for him as he set off up the hill towards the moors: 'When I left the main town centre, within one minute fog came down, and I just couldn't see further than five or six feet in front of the car. You couldn't see any road signs, where you were going at all and my fear at that time was that I would miss the turning. I had no idea how long I had to travel, so I got it in my mind that it was starting to get very late.'

In fact, visibility was so bad that it took Kevin forty-five minutes to get to his next destination. The police were able to speak to him through the transmitter and all the time they were reassuring him that everything would be all right. Finally, he arrived at the phone box. He recalls: 'The telephone box was illuminated, it was very isolated, there was fog swirling around it. It was just like a graveyard and I decided that I would get into the box and out again as quickly as possible.'

He found the message in a brown envelope and carried it back to the car. He read it out aloud: 'THIS ROUTE WILL SHOW IF YOU ARE BEING FOLLOWED.' Little did he realize, however, that as he was doing so, his microphone was breaking up and the police were having difficulty hearing him. They did not always respond to his messages and he was concentrating so hard that he was quite unaware of the situation.

The message told him to turn around, then turn right fifty yards up on the right-hand side, then turn left about a hundred yards on the left-hand side, down a bridle path. As he made the turn, the police lost all radio contact with him. His microphone had gone completely dead; he was now on his own.

Kevin recalls, 'When I turned down the bridle path, the first thing I saw was a Shipways sign, which had been made up – it was a little wooden stake in the ground. I thought he's waiting for me at the end of this track, this is it. This is the crunch. Due to the foggy conditions and the way that he was starting to twist my mind, I was completely oblivious to the fact that communications may have broken down. From my point of view I knew that there was the possibility that they would black out any sort of communication with me if this was going to be the point where the drop was going to take place.'

The road was now just a dirt track, full of divots and holes. Kevin was frightened that the car might break down. As he kept driving, he was thinking aloud, hoping that the police could pick up exactly where he was. He had been told to look for a red and white cone. By the cone was a bag. The message told him to place the money in the bag that was by the cone.

Kevin saw the cone and began to take deep breaths. He recalls, 'Because of the fog, there was walls all the way around, he could have just stepped out and touched me, and I wouldn't have known until he was on top of me. I was extremely, extremely frightened. I didn't want to get out of the car but I just had to grit my teeth. I got the impression that he wanted me to transfer the money out of the car, but in view of the fact that I was so isolated and vulnerable at that time, there was no way I was going to do that.'

Kevin got out of his car, grabbed the bag from underneath the cone and quickly jumped back inside. When he opened the bag, he transferred the money as requested and saw another message inside. There was a stencilled message saying: 'GO TO END OF LANE – TURN LEFT BACK TO ROUNDABOUT (A628/9) TURN RIGHT – PHONE BOX 3.5 MLS LHS MESSAGE TAPED UNDER SHELF 15 mins ALLOWED.'

Kevin could not believe that he had to drive nearly another four miles. He kept wondering what was coming next: 'I was scared. It was terrible. You couldn't put into words how I felt at that point. I was just totally alone with him.'

Meanwhile, Stephanie was waiting inside her coffin and beginning to get even more worried. Her kidnapper had said he would be back between 8 and 9 p.m. He had left that morning around 9.15 a.m. and given her KitKats and a cold drink. He returned around midday and explained that he had a busy afternoon and would not be back until the evening. By 9 p.m. the telephone still had not rung, and she had heard nothing. She remembers, 'I knew that today was the day that he was collecting the money. I feared he had been arrested and that I would not be found. I decided that if he didn't return by midnight I was going to smother my face with the pillow, in an attempt to commit suicide. I was all prepared for this and I recall hearing the 10.30 p.m. news on the radio.'

Kevin knew how much Stephanie's life depended on him carrying out the instructions precisely and, as he carried on along the single track, it was now pitch black and still very foggy. He was driving slowly when, suddenly, right in the middle of his pathway, he saw a cone: 'I was just going along on automatic pilot and when I saw the cone I stopped and tried to read the message that was stuck to it. I didn't want to get out of the car again, but I realized that I would have to. I stooped down and read it in the car headlights.' Again, it was written with stencils. It said: 'ON WALL BY 4 SIGN – WOOD TRAY – DO NOT MOVE TRAY SENSOR INSIDE – PUT MONEY BAG ON TRAY – IF BUZZER DOES NOT SOUND LEAVE MONEY THERE – REMOVE CONE FROM INFRONT OF CAR AND GO – MONEY WILL NOT BE COLLECTED UNTIL YOU HAVE LEFT.'

Kevin recalls, 'At the time, I was just going along with exactly what he was saying. I wasn't in control of my own mind, he was. The feelings I had were indescribable. Once I'd placed all the money on the tray I just wanted to get out of there. I understood afterwards that there was actually a message on the tray, which I didn't pick up, purely and simply because I was in so much of a panic. The message had told me to return to my office and wait for a telephone call which would tell me where Stephanie was.'

After Kevin had dumped the money, he quickly drove out of the area and the police caught up with him as he approached the main road. Detective Chief Superintendent Mick Foster recalls, 'Everything had been going well until we had the technical breakdown. We lost Kevin for a short period of crucial time. When we found him again, we realized that the money had been dropped. I think at that particular time, knowing the money had been dropped, thinking that the kidnapper had then probably escaped, and the realization that we still didn't know whether Stephanie was safe and going to be released, was probably one of the worst moments of my career.'

It was nearly 11 p.m. when Stephanie heard a car. She was frantic with worry and shouted out, 'Did you get the money?' He replied, 'Yes.' She asked if everything went all right and he said, 'Yes, apart from my mate falling off his motor bike three times because of the weather conditions.' While still blindfolded, he led her to a chair where she changed back into her own clothes. He held her arm and guided her into another building, possibly a car port, and she got inside a car. It was freezing cold and, after about two miles, he put the heater on.

Once they realized that they had missed him, the police were desperate to flood the area with officers, but of course this would have been very dangerous, and caused risk to Stephanie's life. So, as the rest of the team were alerted to the night's events, the family liaison officer, who was with Warren and Betty Slater, knew it was going to be a difficult evening. They would need a lot of reassurance and support now. The officer recalled, 'Later that evening, I went upstairs to use the toilet. I just happened to pick the wrong moment. There was a loud banging and ringing, which concerned me greatly. Warren was heading for the door and I shouted to him to leave it and that I'd answer it.'

It was too late – the door was already open and standing there was Stephanie. Everyone was dumbstruck; they could not believe it was really her. Warren remembers, 'I was just in a whirl. I couldn't believe what was going on and that she was in the house. She couldn't believe it herself. She kept pinching herself.' Everyone hugged Stephanie and physically she seemed to be all right. She stayed at home that night, but the next morning, as had already been planned, she was taken to a private hospital where she could be cared for and debriefed. Also to hand were medical facilities in case she might have need of them.

Immediately, the message that Stephanie was back home safe and well was relayed to headquarters. Detective Superintendent Mick Williams recalled, 'I just couldn't believe it, and I thought, right, now the inquiry really starts. If she's back safe and well, we've got something to work to, and at long last he wasn't calling the shots, we were.'

The police began interviewing residents and a neighbour recalled seeing a red Metro car pull up outside his house the previous evening. He remembered a girl getting out backwards, she looked sort of drunk. He was adamant about the colour – vermilion red – a sort of orangey red; he had been a paint sprayer for fifteen years. He was also adamant about the type of car he had seen: it was a Metro.

Police also found where Kevin Watts had dropped off the money. The walls Kevin had seen around him in the fog turned out to be the parapets of a railway bridge. The extortionist had been below on the bed of an abandoned railway line, known as the Dove Valley Trail. It runs to another bridge three miles away, the one where the painted brick and strange container had been found in the Julie Dart case. Here, again, they found a dummy device with silver paint on it. This time, though, instead of a plan to hoist the money up, a length of washing line was used to pull it down.

The news blackout had now ended and, after a meeting between the combined forces of West Midlands and West Yorkshire, it was decided that the Assistant Chief Constable of West Yorkshire, Tom Cook, should take over the whole inquiry. He quickly decided not to give journalists his strongest clue, at least not yet – the tapes of the kidnapper's voice. There were lessons that had been learned from the Yorkshire Ripper case. Thousands of names might be suggested by members of the public and suspects would need to be prioritized, but, first, detectives had to talk to Stephanie, discover gently all the tiny details she could give and build a check-list in preparation for a big appeal. In fact, Stephanie was debriefed over a period of eight days.

As she began recounting her ordeal, the police discovered that she was an extremely easy person to interview. She was very cooperative and she had been able to remember things in great detail. She recalled waking up on the first morning to the sound of Radio 2. A few minutes later, at around 8 a.m., the man returned to the room. He pulled her out of her coffin and she could not believe the agony that she was in. He realized that the box was too small and said he would saw part of it off to make her more comfortable. He offered to make some porridge, and she remembered hearing a ping, which must have been the microwave.

She lay on a mattress for most of that day and remembered hearing voices outside the room, being aware of people coming in and out of the premises holding brief conversations with the man. At some point, she became aware of a dog inside the premises. The man later told her that he had a six-month-old Alsatian bitch.

Her recollection of those days in captivity was that they followed the same routine. She would hear the man leaving in a vehicle each evening, closing the heavy metal door behind him. Each morning she would awake to the sound of the radio at about 8 a.m. He would then get her out of her box and sit her in a chair where she would eat breakfast.

She thought the room was used as some sort of a work area because she often heard the sounds of banging and hammering. The building smelt of damp, oil and grease. On one occasion, the final night of her captivity, the man allowed her to sleep outside her coffin on a mattress. Over the top of her blindfold, she managed to see a single wooden beam on the ceiling. She also remembered hearing a telephone ring, and although it only rang two or three times, she was certain it was an old-fashioned one. Also, from time to time, she heard another bell which sounded a bit like it came from an old-fashioned cash register.

Detective Superintendent Mick Williams recalls, 'The information that was coming in from her was absolutely vital. Her recollection was incredible and we were beginning to put everything together like a jigsaw puzzle.'

Gradually, a picture was beginning to emerge of the man they were looking for, and the place that he operated from. As a result of the information from Stephanie and other enquiries, the police were concentrating on an area in Nottinghamshire. Police had also released an artist's impression of the kidnapper, and had been deluged with calls.

Meanwhile, about a week after Stephanie's release, the kidnapper sent his final letter. He called it 'The Facts'. This was to turn out to be his biggest downfall. It began: 'I, being the kidnapper of Stephanie Slater, am not the killer of Julie Dart. It is impossible that there can be any positive connection between the two cases. I am also not the person who idiotically tried to blackmail BR. The idear was a variation of an idear I had discussed with another, I now believe that he may have used my word processor to make his demands. The reason for the sudden cessation of communications between BR and the other, was my intervention when I learned with horror that he was to use my idears about picking up ransom monies....'

The letter went on to explain how he had dropped Stephanie off, and how sorry he was for what had happened. It was posted in Barnsley on Wednesday 5 February, and copied eight times. Those in receipt included Lynn Dart, West Yorkshire and West Midlands Police, BBC Television, Yorkshire Television, the *News of the World* and *The Sun* newspapers.

The police immediately knew that the letter was genuine. It contained similar spelling mistakes to the earlier Julie Dart letters, and phrases like 'with a little luck' were repeated. It seemed that the author wanted to distance himself from Julie Dart's murder and the British Rail blackmail demand. However, by introducing a friend who supposedly committed these crimes, he, in fact, strengthened the case against him because he had now admitted that there was a link between all three crimes.

The letter seemed to be the start of the killer's defence. Perhaps he felt the police closing in, now that the artist's impression and details about him had been released.

Once Stephanie's debriefing was over and all the available information about her kidnapper had been analysed, a press conference was arranged for Thursday morning, 20 February, and, that evening, *Crimewatch UK* broadcast its special appeal.

Through the appeal, the police were asking the public to put all the clues together and, if anyone knew someone who looked like the artist's impression, sounded like the voice and had a small, red hatchback car, then these names would get priority. Thirty-eight lines were set up in Birmingham and a further twenty at Bradford.

The Assistant Chief Constable Tom Cook recalls, 'I felt this was our main chance. You've got a massive inquiry, we'd had a long investigation in relation to Julie's murder, which you could regard as one bite of the cherry. There'd been the kidnap and the ransom drop, which you could regard as the second bite of the cherry, and we'd got nowhere with those, and, if you like, this was our third bite at the cherry.'

Sitting at home, watching *Crimewatch UK* that night, was Michael Sams and his wife, Teena. Mr Sams remarked to Teena after a few minutes that the kidnapper could almost be him, and she replied, 'It's a good job you've got a tin leg.' He warned her that the police would be checking everyone with a red car, and that if they turned up the next day, or the next month, she should not worry.

About a hundred miles away in Keighley, West Yorkshire, Susan Oake returned home after an evening out. It was about 11 p.m. She had seen all the publicity about the kidnapper and had a strange nagging thought that it just might be her ex-husband Michael Sams. She had seen him only a few days earlier at his father's funeral. He was by nature a secretive, evasive person, but she recalled that he was even more so on this occasion, deliberately avoiding any eye contact. He even refused her a lift in his car, which she thought very odd. Although they had been divorced for fifteen years, she kept in touch with his family.

Michael Sams was driving a red Metro that day, but she had quickly dismissed his involvement in the kidnapping because there had been no mention of his artificial leg. However, for her own peace of mind, she was keen to see *Crimewatch UK*, hear the voice and know for certain that it was not him. She had first suspected his involvement in the crime when her local paper published a Photofit. However, her suspicions were not strong enough to contact the police and, several days later, when details about the railway badge were disclosed, she grew more concerned. However, still nobody mentioned his artificial leg.

That evening, she had gone out and so video taped the programme. As soon as she got in, she sat down to watch and, when she heard the voice, she was stunned.

She immediately leapt up: 'I just went hysterical, I knew it was his voice, and I paced up and down the room twenty or thirty times shouting "It's him!" I just wanted to stop him talking because the more he talked the more I knew it was him.'

Susan could not get through to the studio because the

lines were jammed: over thirteen hundred calls were received that night. Instead, she rang her local police station, Keighley, and was put through to the Millgarth incident room in Leeds. The Stephanie Slater incident room in Birmingham was taking hundreds of calls, but the officers in Leeds were only on standby. They answered just thirteen calls; ironically one of them was from Susan Oake.

Susan gave the name 'Michael Sams' and told the police officer that he had a small red car, ran a small power tools business from a workshop in Newark, and was passionately interested in railways. She then went on to say that Michael Sams had an artificial leg and asked why nobody had mentioned his limp.

Susan then rang her son and asked him to listen to the voice, which was due to be repeated on *Crimewatch Update*. He agreed that the voice and description fitted precisely; it was his father. Apart from Susan, he was the only person to name Michael Sams.

Susan's call was just one of a number that needed to be checked, and officers visited her at home later that evening to take down more details.

Detective Sergeant Tim Grogan was intimately involved with the Julie Dart inquiry. He, along with several others, had been piecing all the information together over seven long months and was desperately hoping for more leads. The day after *Crimewatch* he had arranged a day's leave, but Yorkshire Television had asked him to do an interview, so he had agreed to come in on his day off. When he arrived on Friday morning, Detective Constable Greenwood rushed straight over and said that he had taken a call from a Susan Oake the night before and that she was certain she knew who the kidnapper was. Detective Sergeant Grogan recalls, 'I immediately asked him if it was her ex-husband. He told me that it was. I laughed and dismissed it because I'd already taken about five calls as a result of *Crimewatch* and they'd all said it was an ex-husband. However, he kept nagging me and eventually I asked if the man had got any previous. When we discovered that he had, I asked him to get a photograph. As soon as I saw a picture of Michael Sams I noticed that he had features described by Stephanie so I cancelled my television interview and went to look for him.'

They drove for about an hour before they arrived at Mr Sams' home, 'Eaves Cottage', Sutton-on-Trent. It was about 10.30 a.m. and his wife, Teena, said he was at work, but was due back around 4 p.m. When detectives walked through the door, their eyes were drawn to the railway memorabilia plastered all over the walls. In one room was a word processor, in another a fish tank and, finally, outside was an Alsatian dog. However, not wanting to alert Teena to their suspicions, they said that they would return later in the afternoon, but, in the meantime, could she tell them where his workplace was? Armed with this information, they quickly left. They had been in the house for only five minutes.

Teena explained that Michael Sams worked at T and M Tools in Newark. His workshop backed on to the River Trent and to one side was Newark Castle. They were anxious to get there as soon as possible. Detective Sergeant Tim Grogan recalls, 'As we approached his premises, everything was just as Stephanie had described it. Her recollection was excellent. She remembered as he drove her to the door going down a slope which bore left. She walked from the car to the door and recalled wind blowing on her face. We did the same, the wind was coming from the alleyway. The red Metro was parked in exactly the right place. The name T and M Tools was written in stencil, like a number of the letters we'd received and, more importantly, it said "Closed Wednesday". This was crucial because all his activities had taken place on a Wednesday: the day the letters were posted, the phone calls made, and the ransom collected.'

When they went inside, they had to open a heavy wooden door that was on sliding metal runners – again, just as Stephanie had remembered. Inside was a large room divided into sections: a front showroom, a counter area, a small utility room and, at the back, a dark, dingy storage area. Above, on the ceiling, was a single wooden beam. Detective Sergeant Grogan shouted out, 'Is anybody there?' A small, greasy haired man with a limp, wearing blue overalls, appeared. Tim Grogan recalls, 'I couldn't believe that this was him. I was expecting to see some ex-SAS officer trained in surveillance. Yet, standing in front of me, was a shambling, one-legged, trainspotter.'

The detectives looked around the room and saw an old telephone, a microwave and the radio, which was tuned to Radio 2. The only thing that was not apparent was the old till. It was only when the door opened that a bell sounded, then everything tied in precisely with how Stephanie had described it.

Michael Sams was arrested and taken to Newark police station. Once inside, he appeared pale and distressed and, just prior to being placed in the cells, he confessed to the kidnap: 'I kidnapped Stephanie Slater, but I didn't murder Julie Dart – you'll find £19000 at the workshop with my confession.' He knew his workshop was going to be thoroughly checked and that detectives would find the money.

Michael Benniman Sams was born in Keighley, West Yorkshire, in 1941. He went to Riddlesden Church of England School, where he excelled in most subjects, except English. His spelling was poor and it was later believed that he suffered from a form of dyslexia. He passed his eleven-plus and, after gaining passes in O and A levels, he went on to study at Hull Nautical College. When he was nineteen he joined the Merchant Navy and, for three years, he travelled the world. Then, in the early 1960s, he returned to Keighley where he worked for Keighley Lifts and, several years later, in 1967, he started his own central heating business. Mr Sams met his first wife, Susan Oake, in 1962 and, two years later, they were married. Susan was just twenty and they moved to a house in Oakworth, Keighley. Six years later, their first child was born and, in 1970, they had a second son.

Michael Sams was a keen athlete and, for many years, had been a member of Bingley Harriers, his local club. He enjoyed cross country running and had completed the arduous Three Peaks Race on more than one occasion. From time to time, he developed problems with his knee, when the tendons became inflamed. Tests later revealed that he had a growth, but this was not malignant. He was also interested in DIY and car maintenance, but his biggest love was trains; he had spent thousands of pounds on railway memorabilia.

During the early 1970s, Mr Sams' business was going very well. The family moved into a large, detached house and he was working long hours. Then, a few years later, in about 1974, he was struck by a sudden illness. At first it was thought that he had meningitis, but tests proved inconclusive. However, Mr Sams seemed to undergo a personality change, and furious rows followed and he became violent towards his wife. As a result, the marriage came under considerable strain and, three years later, they were divorced.

There followed a long and bitter row over maintenance payments and it seemed that Mr Sams was struggling to make ends meet. Around this time, he became involved with the police because of a stolen car he was driving. He was infatuated with MGBs and, one day, the police were doing routine checks on vehicles when they stopped him and discovered that the car he was driving had been stolen. In 1978 he was sent to prison for six months for the theft.

Prior to his prison sentence, a fire had been started deliberately at his house and it caused extensive damage.

It was while he was repairing the landing window that he fell and injured his right knee. This aggravated his problem and, while in prison, his condition deteriorated. Doctors diagnosed cancer and the only chance he had was to have his leg amputated.

It was while he was in prison that he started seeing Jane. They had met through the personal column of a newspaper when he was on bail awaiting trial. During his sentence their relationship deepened and, a few weeks after his release, they were married. The marriage lasted for only three years.

At this time, the Black and Decker Tool Company, for whom he worked, was reducing staff in Leeds and Mr Sams was asked if he would transfer to Birmingham. He was now single and had no ties so was happy to accept the move.

Once in Birmingham, he answered another lonely hearts advertisement in the paper and met Teena, who was to become his third wife. Mr Sams then started his own company, Peterborough Power Tools, and, after that, T and M Tools in Newark. It was here that he kept Stephanie Slater.

Once he had been arrested for abducting her, he was interviewed by West Midlands police and, two days later, he was returned to Leeds. Detective Sergeant Tim Grogan began interviewing him: 'He was so arrogant at this time. He wanted all the glory for abducting Stephanie. He thought he was so successful, carrying out everything as he'd planned. He felt a real celebrity. To admit killing Julie Dart was to admit failure, and he was very unhappy about being interviewed here in Leeds. He hated Leeds.'

'I can categorically state I never knew Julie Dart, I've never seen her or talked to her.'
'We believe you held Julie in your workshop.'
'No, there's no truth in that. I didn't have anything to

do with Julie Dart, and what I'm waiting for is the evidence that links the two cases together.'

As soon as Michael Sams was arrested, his workshop was sealed off and the long search for forensic evidence began. Detective Superintendent Bob Taylor recalls, 'It must have gone through Sams' mind that we were going to find evidence that would link him with the Julie Dart murder, because next morning he called for the interviewing officers and he changed his story.' He said, 'One of the things I said at the start that no one has picked up is that £20 000 was for another's help. Well, on the Wednesday, an accomplice picked me up and took me to all the boxes where I left the messages and telephoned Kevin Watts. Then he took me to the bridge where the money was to be dropped and left me there. After that everything was exactly as I described it. I drove along the Dove Valley Trail back to where the car was parked, and we set off back to my workshop. On the way an argument developed with this other person.'

Mr Sams then appeared very distressed and his solicitor offered to read out a statement he had prepared earlier that morning: 'As we were driving along I said, "Christ, I've forgotten to fill my car up, I won't make it to Birmingham and back." My partner replied, "What the hell are you on about, we're going to kill her now and I'll dispose of the body," I being the other man. I thought he was joking. I said she's going home. "No she isn't," he said, "she'll identify you." A heated argument broke out in which I received a cut to my wrist from a knife he had. I was adamant that Stephanie wouldn't identify me, but this did not satisfy him. In the end I agreed to give him all the money, except around £20 000, not to identify him, and not to tell the police where the money was until I had been charged.'

Mr Sams had wanted all the glory himself, but suddenly he had to blame someone else, and so invented his 'accomplice'. The police's immediate response to this new story was 'Name the man', but Mr Sams had thought that one through and replied, 'I can't because if I did he might take it out on someone else, on Stephanie herself, and I wouldn't want to take that risk.'

The police believed that this new story, invented by Mr Sams, was a convenient way for him to explain away any evidence that they had to connect him with Julie Dart's murder. Detective Sergeant Tim Grogan recalls, 'It was significant that he was accepting at this stage that we'd got a substantial amount of evidence and he'd got to create this second person to accept some of the darker facts that were emerging.'

The evidence was indeed beginning to build up. Mr Sams had installed electricity in his shop and fitted an alarm system that incorporated infra-red detectors (PIR). The positioning of them ensured that anyone moving around inside the shop would be detected. They were connected to an alarm control box, and the wiring was arranged in such a way that when they detected movement, no noise would be heard at the workshop; instead the phone would ring at Mr Sams' house. It was only eight minutes' drive away. This proved that Mr Sams was technically minded and, in the Julie Dart letters, the author indicated that he had a detector to ensure there was no bug or transmitter in the ransom package. A similar letter had also been written in connection with the Slater inquiry. Also, stencilling was common to both inquiries, as was the Dove Valley Trail.

However, Mr Sams was still denying any involvement with the Julie Dart murder or the British Rail blackmail demand. The day after his arrest, he agreed to give a sample of his handwriting and this was sent away for comparison with the letters received earlier in the inquiry.

Meanwhile, at Mr Sams' workshop, forensic experts had found, among other things, a long strand of hair and an old curtain that had a blood stain on it. The hair could have come from Stephanie, but there were also some hairs that could have come from Julie Dart. The watery blood stain on the bottom of the curtain appeared to have soaked in when someone was cleaning up. This blood was subsequently shown to be of the same group as Julie's, and different to that of Michael Sams, his wife and Stephanie Slater. Some mustard-coloured tufts of carpet fibres found turned out to be indistinguishable from the fibres and tufts recovered from the sheet and rope that had been used to wrap up Julie's body.

Back in the interview room, the police put to Mr Sams details that had emerged from the final letter, 'The Facts' letter, posted a week after Stephanie's release. Mr Sams had admitted writing this letter. However, he continually denied any involvement with the other crimes, saying that they were not linked.

'In a previous letter, you said that you know the man that murdered Julie Dart, and tried to extort money from British Rail.'
'That's correct.'
'Is this the same man that's got all the money from the Slater kidnap, your accomplice?'
'It is, yes.'
'But you've always said that these cases could never be linked with the Stephanie Slater case, you've always been adamant about that.'
'Yes.'
'But now you're saying the cases are linked?'
'Now they can be linked.'

It was with a certain amount of arrogance that Mr Sams finally made this admission. It was the first time he had accepted that the cases were linked, and this was to prove very important. Detective Superintendent Bob Taylor recalls, 'Before, he hadn't been prepared to answer any direct questions about the Julie Dart murder, but in linking the cases himself, he'd backed down. He exuded a sense of superiority. He wouldn't accept facts that were presented to him unless they came from an expert, and that soon became the area on which we concentrated.'

Once detectives had all the information from the forensic expert regarding the mustard-coloured tufts of carpet fibres that matched those found on the shroud wrapped around Julie, they questioned him at length. He replied:

'Impossible for them to be the same.'
'So what explanation can you give?'
'I say it's impossible.'
'But forensically if it proves...'
'Yes. Yes.'
'What are you going to say then?'
'I'm not going to change my story one bit.'

That, though, is exactly what he did. Having finished the interview, he would go away, think about it, realize he could not get away with his explanation, and come back with a different story, which usually involved the other man. This he did time and time again.

When questioned about the carpet fibres in his workshop again, he explained that the sheet and rope must have been there, but his accomplice took them.

He was then interviewed in detail about the handwritten letters. The expert, having analysed the letters written in the Julie Dart inquiry and the sample of Michael Sams' own handwriting, was certain that he was the author of the letters. Detective Sergeant Tim Grogan began:

'Those samples have been examined by a forensic scientist and it is his opinion that you wrote the York letter and the Conventry one.'
'Well, I thought that's what you were going to lead up

*to, but I definitely didn't write them, I'll always main-
tain that.'*

'The forensic scientist is a handwriting expert.'

'No. I'm sorry.'

'He's examined them and said you wrote them.'

'Well, if he's right he's right, but I say I didn't.'

*'There are fourteen identical spelling mistakes. How do
you account for that?'*

'I've no explanation at all.'

Once again, after Mr Sams had finished this interview,
he went away, thought about it and then changed his
story. Detective Sergeant Grogan was stunned when
Michael Sams finally admitted writing the letters: 'I
couldn't believe it. It seemed he was frightened of
experts and never disputed anything they said.' Mr Sams
began:

'I did write them. I told you a lie.'

'So you did write the letters.'

*'Yes I did. I was used, he made me write them, he was
using me for a pillock.'*

'But why did you do it?'

'It seemed like a good idea at the time.'

*'But you must have known he'd killed someone, it's in
the letters you now admit you wrote?'*

'What difference does that make?'

*'Doesn't the cold-blooded murder of a young girl have
any effect on you?'*

*'No. I'd never like to think that I'd killed her in my
mind. I'd not like to think that. I don't care what the
rest of the world thinks.'*

The evidence against Mr Sams was now overwhelming:

- he had finally admitted to writing the letters
- fibres from his workshop matched those found with
  Julie's body

- a computer found in his home had information on it relating to a prostitute called 'Julie D', along with details relating to the British Rail blackmail, and the Stephanie Slater kidnap (Mr Sams thought he had deleted these files, but experts had managed to retrieve them)

- silver paint was common in both cases: first, on the device found on the M1, which was later blown up, and, second, on the device left at the pick-up point in relation to the Stephanie Slater inquiry (this type of paint was distributed mainly through railway model shops and samples were traced back to a shop in Newark, then tests revealed that it was the same as that found on Mr Sams' motorcycle and a water tank that he had painted; it was also in the attic on part of his model railway set).

However, much as detectives questioned Mr Sams about the invention of his 'accomplice', saying that it was just another part of his game plan, on this subject his story never changed. It was his main defence. If detectives could only find the rest of the money, then, with luck, it would destroy this part of his story once and for all.

In the months that followed the arrest of Michael Sams, the investigation team had been unable to put Mr Sams anywhere near Julie's body. The nearest they got was Grantham, which was seven miles away. They started going back through all the witnesses' statements once again, and it was here that they discovered a farmer who had seen a red car near to where Julie's body was found. He was re-interviewed and, although he could not describe the man himself, he recalled two other witnesses who could.

These witnesses were interviewed and remembered that the man limped and had a stick. This information was put to Mr Sams, but he denied it all. So, an identification parade was arranged and the witnesses called.

Unfortunately, they failed to pick him out, but afterwards Mr Sams did admit to being near there. The area was called Stoke Summit; just 1½ miles from where Julie Dart's body was found. Detective Sergeant Grogan recalls, 'He just couldn't help himself. He thought he'd got nothing to lose, and he loved the sound of his own voice. He was just leading us along.'

Once he had admitted being in the area, detectives asked him what he was doing there. He said he was trainspotting on a Wednesday, some time after Stephanie had been released. He even remembered what the weather was like – dull and raining. Armed with this new information, detectives began looking in detail at everything Sams had told them. As they analysed it more and more, they could not understand why he would go trainspotting on a rainy day, especially on the East Coast Line, which ran next to his house; he could have seen the trains from his own front window.

It seemed that he was helping detectives more than he realized. Detective Sergeant Tim Grogan recalls, 'We checked the weather forecast for the day he said he'd visited the area and the only date it could have been was Wednesday 19 February, the day before *Crimewatch UK*. My suspicions were immediately aroused and, going on the theory that he knew the television appeal was about to happen, and we were closing in on him, he had wanted to move the money. My hunch was that this was where he had buried it.'

Mr Sams had always denied burying it at home. There was a hole at the side of his house and he said that he had prepared the hole, but had never used it because the other man did not want it buried there. Detectives felt sure that this was just another fabricated story and that if they discounted the second man, it was obvious that Mr Sams had moved the cash. Going on the theory that the place he would choose would be isolated yet familiar, so that nobody else would be able to find it,

Stoke Summit seemed to be the ideal spot.

Special ground-probing radar equipment was booked from Aberdeen to search the area. This was expensive, but effective. It fires sonic beams into the soil and an echo sound is transferred back to the operator, detecting whether anything solid is below. The area they were looking at was vast and Detective Superintendent Bob Taylor recalls, 'We'd identified a number of likely places where it could be and, working on the principle that he would have to have a fixed point – a tree, a post or something – to be able to identify where he'd buried it, that was where we began to work.'

The search started on Tuesday and the equipment was booked for three days. Detectives felt certain that the money was there somewhere, but they were not confident that they would find it in the short time available. However, on the final day, when spirits were flagging, a shout came up and eight inches below the surface, they found a box. Packaged in a Black and Decker parts tray, about the size of a seed tray, was the money. Identical trays had been found in Mr Sams' workshop and a similar one had been given to Stephanie to use as a toilet (he had no running water on the premises).

Detectives were delighted and thought that finally they had won the game. The package was sent, unopened, for forensic examination.

However, the following morning, Michael Sams had read about the discovery in the papers and asked detectives to visit him. He told them, 'You've only found half of it.'

On hearing this news, they were very dejected because this still left open the possibility that the other man, 'the accomplice', had the other half. After checking with the forensic scientist, their fears were confirmed – only half the money was there. This had been packaged up in a certain way, exactly the same as the killer of Julie Dart had requested, and all the £50 notes were missing.

Detective Sergeant Tim Grogan recalls, 'Sams told us that the other man had buried the rest of the money, but it was in close proximity. Again, he was enjoying manipulating us and leading us along. The special ground-probing radar equipment had gone back to Aberdeen, so there was nothing more we could do other than get down there and start digging. I was frightened the press might discover what had happened and be at the scene before us, looking for the money. So, at 7 a.m. sharp, we went to Stoke Summit.'

Again, the area that they were looking at was vast, but after only three hours they found a patch of soft ground sixteen feet away from the first find. When one of the men stuck the fork into the ground, out came the money. It was packaged in an ice cream carton and placed inside a Black and Decker bag bearing the advertisement 'We know how. Do you know where?'

For Detective Superintendent Bob Taylor and his team, it was one of the greatest moments of the whole inquiry; it completely destroyed the theory of an 'accomplice'. If there *had* been a second man, he had had plenty of opportunity to have gone back and collected the money.

During the past eighteen months since his arrest, West Yorkshire police had compiled a substantial case against Michael Sams, who was still denying the murder of Julie Dart. His only defence remained the 'other' man. Charged with blackmailing British Rail, the abduction and kidnap of Stephanie Slater and the murder of Julie Dart, the prosecution case lasted for nearly three weeks. Among those called to give evidence were Stephanie Slater and Mr Sams' ex-wife, Susan Oake. Stephanie described in detail her terror, the wooden box she had slept inside and the outer container, the wheely bin, that had been her bed.

In his defence, Mr Sams gave evidence, but again he refused to name his 'accomplice' and still he maintained his innocence in connection with Julie Dart's death. On Thursday 8 July 1993, after retiring for just three hours, the jury returned their verdict.

Michael Sams was found guilty on every charge and given four life sentences. The judge, in his summing up, said, 'When Stephanie Slater was kidnapped, I have not the slightest doubt that she was in desperate and mortal danger, and if it had seemed necessary to you she, like Julie Dart, would have been murdered in cold blood. Her survival, in my judgement, is entirely due to her own remarkable moral courage, and the unostentatious display of qualities of character that have excited the admiration and respect of everyone in this court, from the jury to the judge.'

Once in prison, just four days after the trial, Michael Sams summoned detectives to his prison cell. Finally, two years after her death, Michael Sams admitted killing Julie Dart. He had seen a newspaper article that showed Lynn Dart beside Julie's grave, but the headstone had no date. Detective Superintendent Bob Taylor recalls, 'He said that he just wanted to tell us what had happened to Julie, and the date that he'd killed her. It was Wednesday 10 July, the day after he had picked her up. He said that when he struck her, it was from behind and she knew nothing about it. His explanation was very matter of fact, and he showed no remorse.'

2

THE RED CONNECTION

etective Chief Superintendent Jack Taylor was just
getting into bed when the telephone rang. It was the
Duty Inspector, David Hitch. He had been called to
a cottage in the grounds of the Rothay Manor Hotel,
Ambleside, to investigate a suspicious death. When he
arrived, he found the body of a woman lying face
upwards in the bathroom. Telephone cable was round
her ankles and wrists, and over her head was a plastic
bag secured with a scarf and white multicable flex.

It was the early hours of Tuesday 21 January 1986
when Detective Chief Superintendent Jack Taylor arrived
at the scene. The dead woman was quickly identified as
Bronwen Nixon, a well-respected hotel proprietor. Now
there was no doubt in anyone's mind that this was murder, but who would want to kill her, and in such a brutal way? The pathologist was called and arrangements
were made to begin a thorough search of the house.

Cumbria is the second largest county in England. It
stretches from the Scottish borders to the edge of
Lancashire and spans 2653 square miles. Throughout
the night Detective Inspector Hitch had the arduous task
of rounding up an inquiry team from the county's four
divisions, each on-call detective was contacted and asked
to provide at least three officers. The area surrounding
the hotel needed to be combed for clues, and it was
important for house-to-house enquiries to start as soon

as possible. Experts in this area are the task force, so a further twenty officers were drafted in.

Detective Chief Superintendent Jack Taylor arranged for an incident room to be set up at Kendal police station and he was keen to hold a 9 a.m. briefing. He wanted to start early so that officers could begin immediately checking bus and railway stations and implementing road checks to see if anyone had seen anything suspicious that night.

Bronwen Muriel Gwendoline Nixon was born in Huddersfield in 1918. She was sixty-seven when she died and had owned the Rothay Manor Hotel for the past eighteen years. She originally bought the hotel in 1967 with three partners, but two had died and she bought the third one out in 1975. By this time she had also bought Lee Cottage, which is in the hotel grounds, and had lived there for the past six years.

Bronwen had been divorced for about twenty-five years and had two grown-up sons, Nigel and Stephen. After leaving Leeds University, Nigel returned to Ambleside to help his mother run the business. About the same time, Stephen decided to do the same, so, in the late 1970s, a joint ownership agreement was drawn up. Bronwen remained responsible for the kitchen, decor and furnishings of the hotel, Nigel was in charge of all the administration and Stephen looked after the dining room, wines and staff timetable.

During the past five years, Bronwen had become less involved in the day-to-day running of the kitchen, leaving the job to her sons, who had now married and lived nearby. Bronwen Nixon's son Stephen had discovered her body in the bathroom and called the police.

The post mortem was carried out in the early hours of the morning and at 9 a.m. prompt, the briefing began. Detective Chief Superintendent Jack Taylor stood up and opened the meeting: 'In the early hours of this morning, I was called out to the cottage in the grounds of the Rothay Manor Hotel. A woman's body had been discovered whom we now know to be Mrs Bronwen Nixon. What we're looking at is a clear case of murder. The body was found at 22.45 hours yesterday evening, and the cause of death was strangulation. The doctor estimates that she had already been dead for at least twelve hours. She suffered an awful attack. There was bruising around the left eye, a scratch on the right side of the neck, and a cut on her neck. Bruising was also visible by her left collar bone and on both her wrists.

'There are a number of key areas which we must look at:

- how had her attacker got into the house? (there was no sign of forced entry)
- why had her attacker gone into the house – what was the motive?
- there was evidence of theft – there was no sign of Bronwen's purse or its contents, which included credit cards, money and personal papers, but the violence seemed very extreme for robbery
- there was no evidence of any sexual assault
- Bronwen's car – a blue Honda Accord – is missing.

'So, did Bronwen die because she recognized her attacker or did the killer have some specific grudge against her, which might explain the horrific attack he subjected her to? We need to talk to everyone who knew Bronwen. All the employees at the hotel and everyone in the surrounding neighbourhood. The scenes of crime officers are at the cottage looking for any forensic evidence.'

It quickly transpired, after speaking to Bronwen's son, Stephen, that the Rothay Manor Hotel had closed on Sunday 5 January 1986 for its winter break. The day after had been the staff party at The Wordsworth Hotel in Grasmere and, following this, most of them had taken a holiday. The hotel was due to reopen on Friday 14

February, when all the redecoration and repair work had been carried out.

After the staff party, Nigel Nixon went on holiday to the West Indies, Stephen Nixon stayed at home to look after the hotel and Bronwen took a short break. She had gone to London. She stayed for a few days with a friend. She wanted to do some shopping and see the *Nutcracker* at the Festival Hall.

On her return, because the hotel was closed, she had planned to spend more time on her hobbies. One of these was painting, and she would go sketching with a friend called John.

Bronwen had known John and his wife for about thirteen years. They had met through mutual friends, and sometimes John and his wife stayed at the hotel. From time to time, John and Bronwen arranged painting expeditions; she was an expert on both the geography and history of the Lake District.

Bronwen usually selected a subject, and they would then travel to that area to sketch and colour it. She was careful to choose somewhere that was not too far away from the car because of her two dogs. They were called Hoodie and Snug, and the only break she had from painting was to take them for a walk.

John and Bronwen had arranged to go painting on Sunday 19 January. John lived in Saddleworth, near Manchester, and the journey to Ambleside took about an hour and a half. He arrived at the cottage about 10.50 a.m. and Bronwen made a cup of tea. About an hour later, they set off in John's car, taking the dogs with them.

It was quite an overcast day, but the forecast said it was going to improve. They were lucky and the rain stayed away. They painted for most of the day until the light began to fade. Then they drove back to Bronwen's cottage around 4.30 p.m. John remembers, 'We had a cup of tea and compared our day's work. Bronwen remarked that we had not done a sky today, an exercise she was particularly keen on. We examined the sky, which was very dramatic from the studio window. However, this didn't prove to be a very good vantage point because of the trees, so she suggested we sketch it from the picture window in her bedroom. This we did for about fifteen minutes, but it was getting too dark. We then went downstairs and spent a fair amount of time planning our sketching expeditions during the forthcoming year. I left at 5.45 p.m. and, as it had started to rain a little, I suggested to Bronwen not to come out to the car, but she insisted and saw me off as I manoeuvred out of the yard. I arrived home about 7.30 p.m.

'The following morning, I realized that I had left my tweed dales hat in Bronwen's cottage and I had found one of her dog leads in my car so I decided to ring her up. I tried to ring about 2 p.m. but couldn't get any reply. I was then detained at work and didn't leave the office until 9. p.m. I went for a drink and returned home about 10.30 p.m. My wife said that Stephen Nixon had been on the phone, asking if I knew where his mother was. I rang back and spoke to his wife and told her that I had last seen Bronwen on Sunday evening. I asked Stephen's wife to phone me later if there was any news. On Tuesday 21 January, I rang Stephen at 8.30 a.m. He told me that his mother was dead.'

This was the first witness police had spoken to who admitted being with Bronwen Nixon several hours before her death. Because of this, he was initially treated as a suspect because, as far as they were concerned, he was the last person to have seen Bronwen alive. He was arrested and taken to Kendal police station where he was detained for fifteen hours. After details of his story were checked out he was eliminated.

The forensic team, who were making a detailed examination of the cottage, had found blood staining in the hallway. There were clear signs that a struggle had taken place downstairs – items had been knocked over – and this suggested that the attack had begun initially downstairs and then continued upstairs. On the lavatory lid they found a glove mark that was lifted on to Sellotape for analysis. Of even greater significance was a relatively large number of distinctive red cashmere fibres found on and around the body. There was nothing in the house that could account for these.

Detective Chief Superintendent Jack Taylor recalls, 'So far this was the strongest clue we had. Nearly all the hotel staff were away on holiday and only one neighbour had given us any useful information. She lived just down the road from the hotel and at about 11.30 p.m. on the Sunday evening, she had heard a scream. When she went outside to have a look, there was nobody there. All the people we interviewed spoke very highly of Bronwen Nixon, and nobody could think of a reason why anyone would want to kill her.'

Bronwen was in reasonable health at the time of her death. Some years ago she had suffered a heart attack and had quite recently had an attack of angina. Prior to her death, friends said she was quite tired, but this was not surprising as she had been involved in all the Christmas and New Year festivities.

Bronwen was a popular member of the local community. She attended her local church weekly and had many hobbies. She had taken up painting some years ago as a form of relaxation after her heart attack and was recognized in the area for her works of Lakeland scenes. She took part in other local activities, one of which was organizing, with others, the restoration of a platform at Windermere railway station. She also had a keen interest in music and attended many concerts.

In fact, everyone the police spoke to had only respect for Bronwen Nixon and trying to find anyone who held a grudge against her was proving impossible. How, then, were they going to find someone who hated her enough to commit such a violent attack?

Two days after Bronwen's body was found, the incident room received a call from Preston police station. They had found Bronwen's blue Honda Accord in a multistorey car park near the bus station. The only indication as to how long it had been there was an excess charge ticket on the windscreen.

Between 8 a.m. Friday and 6.30 p.m. Sunday, parking is free. The excess ticket had been issued at 11.55 a.m. Monday morning, and a security man who had been on duty the previous evening, Sunday, said that when he had checked the car park, between 10.30 p.m. and 11.02 p.m., the car was definitely not there.

If the killer had parked Bronwen's car in the multistorey, then it is not surprising that it was not there late Sunday evening. Police now believed that it was around this time that Bronwen was killed. Her body was not found until Monday night, but the pathologist had said that she had been dead for at least twelve hours, and from the account given by different witnesses, especially Stephen Nixon, it now seemed more than likely that she had met her death on the Sunday evening.

Stephen Nixon had last seen his mother alive on Saturday 18 January. He had been at the hotel with his wife from around 12 noon to 4 p.m. He then left to play a game of squash. Around 5 p.m. Bronwen drove Stephen's wife home and later that evening Bronwen went to a fundraising concert in Preston for the Liverpool Philharmonic Orchestra.

Stephen knew his mother was going painting on the Sunday morning and saw both her blue Honda and John's white Cortina parked outside the cottage around lunchtime. Stephen was not working that day and had seen the cars when he had driven past.

The next day, Monday 20 January, Stephen arrived at the hotel around 9.45 a.m. He noticed that his mother's car was not there, but thought she must have gone out shopping or was visiting friends. He was not unduly concerned. The two dogs were outside. One was roaming around and the other was tied up in its kennel. This was unusual because Bronwen did not normally tether the dog until about 10 p.m.

Stephen had a key for the cottage and decided to have a quick look round. He let himself in by the back door. He walked round the kitchen, but did not notice anything amiss. He went into the living room and had a quick look around; again, everything seemed to be in order. He noticed that a stool in the hall was lying on its side, but assumed that the dogs had knocked it over. He then left. He did not expect to find his mother there because her car was missing.

That morning he worked in his office, which is opposite the cottage. He finished around lunchtime and went home. He called back at the hotel around 1.30 p.m. and noticed that the dog was still tied up. This time he did not go into the cottage, but when he drove past again at 5 p.m. he noticed that there were still no lights on. Thinking that his mother was still out he decided to call back later.

At 7.30 p.m., Stephen went back to the cottage. He let himself in through the same door and had a good look around the kitchen to see if there was any note, but he could not find one. He then went back into the living room to see if he could find a note on her desk. He switched on the lights and noticed that the room lights had been turned down to a dim glow. This was something Bronwen never did. When he walked back through the hall he noticed the vacuum cleaner; it was not in its usual position.

By now he was beginning to get worried, so decided to take her dogs home with him and ring up John, who had been painting with Bronwen on Sunday, to ask whether he knew her whereabouts. Unfortunately, John was out, and Stephen could only leave a message.

About three hours later, Stephen returned to the cottage with the dogs. Still there was no sign of his mother. He fed the dogs, tied one of them up outside, locked the door and set off back home. On the way, he remembered his wife saying that it might be helpful if he looked in his mother's diary to see if it explained her whereabouts. So he went back to the cottage: 'As I went back to the cottage it occurred to me that I hadn't looked upstairs. I immediately went up the stairs and noticed that her bedroom was in disarray. I looked in the bathroom and saw my mother lying on the bathroom floor. I had to push the door open as she was lying behind it. I saw that she had been tied up. I turned her over and she appeared dead. I immediately left the cottage and went to Ambleside police station. Unfortunately it was closed. The phone in the cottage and hotel were not working because of the alterations, so I used a nearby public telephone box to call the police.'

Once Stephen had been interviewed and Bronwen's car had been found, it was important for the police to find anyone who had seen it, especially between Sunday evening and Monday morning. Local appeals were made for witnesses to come forward.

The car, meanwhile, had been taken away for forensic examination, and the only noticeable difference to it was that the driver's seat was pulled much closer to the steering wheel than normal. Also, the back seat rest, which was usually kept folded down on to the seat, was now in an upright position.

However, the most significant finding was sixteen red cashmere fibres on the driver's seat – identical to those found on Bronwen's body. Detective Chief Superintendent Jack Taylor recalls, 'We didn't know where they had come from, but to find matching alien fibres both on Bronwen's body and in the car was too great a coincidence to ignore. They began to take on an increased significance and we could find neither friend nor family with anything to match them. It seemed more and more likely that they had come from her killer.'

Meanwhile, a number of witnesses came forward as a result of the police appeals, saying that they had seen Bronwen's car. One man was driving to work between 6.50 a.m. and 7 a.m. on Monday 20 January when he had seen the car: 'I drove from my house to the A6 Garstang Road, and as I pulled out on to the Garstang Road, intending to turn right to travel towards North Road, I was forced to give way to a car. It drove past me and I pulled out behind it. When it stopped at the traffic lights, it was in the outside lane and I pulled up along-side it in the nearside lane. I got the impression that somebody was looking at me and I looked across and saw the driver. I immediately noticed his eyes which were staring straight at me. He was about twenty-five to thirty-five years old and had dark, collar-length hair. He was unshaven.'

The witness did not recall the registration number of the car, but noticed it was an old-style Honda Accord, blue in colour.

It was now about a week into the inquiry and the team were having a certain amount of success. A search for evidence continued in Preston while back at Rothay Manor, the hotel's staff were being interviewed. Although the hotel was closed for renovations and most of the staff had gone home, some twenty miles away a waiter, having heard about the murder, contacted the police. He had a chilling feeling that he might know who the killer was: a man who had stayed with him in the staff quarters of the hotel: 'As soon as I heard that Mrs Nixon had been murdered, my gut feeling was that he'd done it, deep down, yet I didn't want to believe it. I mean she's my boss and we got on really well and I was going back to the hotel and they'd offered me a better position at the hotel. But deep down, because of the way he'd treated me, just that he was so violent, and the things he'd said about Mrs Nixon, I felt deep down that he'd done it.'

The waiter was called Andrew and he had worked as a restaurant assistant at the Rothay Manor for about a year. About two months before the murder, on one of his nights off, he had gone with friends to a night-club in Blackpool called the Flamingo Club. While there, he had met a man. This man was called David Wynne Roberts. He was slim, about six feet tall and had dark, almost black, collar-length hair. He also had a very big moustache. Andrew recalls: 'He travelled back with us all to Ambleside and stayed with me in my room. Although most of the staff knew I didn't think the owners did. During the time he stayed he was drawing money from the DHSS. He was with me until Thursday January 9th, apart from two weeks when he went back to Blackpool. During the time he stayed I kept telling him that it was difficult but he made no attempt to leave. It was when I was telling him to go that he became more violent. On one occasion I received a black eye and bruised nose. I never complained to the police because I didn't want to involve the hotel.'

Andrew told the police that David Wynne Roberts used to dye his hair black. He had a distinctive Mexican moustache that he was very proud of and would only shave it off as a last resort. He wore a silver ring on his wedding finger, which had been handed down to him by a member of his family, and a very thin, gold bracelet that had a faulty catch. He drank beer, but only in halves, and he smoked quite a lot. He was also quite a show off, saying he knew famous people, and that he owned a sports car.

David Wynne Roberts told Andrew that he came from near Holyhead, Anglesey, and had left home at the age of fourteen. He did not have any noticeable accent, but spoke quite quickly, which sometimes made it appear that he was being quite sharp with people. He claimed to have lived and worked in London for a time. He also said that he had lived in Brighton.

Andrew told police that during the time they were together, David Wynne Roberts became very possessive towards him and would not let him mix with other staff members. They began having arguments: 'He was quite frankly getting on my nerves. It ended one night when he hit me, not a punch, more a slap, which caused a black eye and a bruised nose. As he got more and more possessive I got more and more frightened of him, and sometimes he even stood in front of the door stopping me from going out.'

The night of the staff party, Monday 6 January, they had an argument. David Wynne Roberts initially said Andrew could not go to the party, but eventually relented and, while Andrew was out celebrating, David Wynne Roberts stayed in his room.

Andrew wanted to go home the next day, but David Wynne Roberts insisted that he stay at the hotel: 'I didn't really know how to handle the situation so I just sat tight until I could sort something out. I finally made up my mind to go home alone on Thursday January 9th. At about 9.30 that morning I rang my father to ask him to come and help me move all my stuff. I also told him that I had this friend staying who wouldn't let me go. I never went back to my room after making that phone call, but stayed in reception.'

David Wynne Roberts had been very angry that morning when Andrew said he was leaving, but eventually he had calmed down and was almost pleading with Andrew to stay with him. After he left, Andrew noticed that £75 and some clothing were missing from his room.

It was eleven days later when Andrew heard from David Wynne Roberts again. At about 7.30 p.m., he rang saying he was in Blackpool, had got a job in London and wanted to meet up to return the clothing he had taken. David Wynne Roberts suggested that they meet in Kendal.

Andrew went with his father. It was just before 10 p.m. when they got to the car park behind the hotel where they had arranged to meet. It was half an hour later before Andrew eventually found David Wynne Roberts, who had been waiting round at the *front* of the building. He returned Andrew's clothes and said he wanted to talk. He said he had nowhere to stay. Andrew gave him the name of a guest house and left with his father. He did not want to get involved.

The following morning, David Wynne Roberts rang Andrew again. It was 9 a.m. and he said he had stayed out all night in Kendal and wanted desperately to meet up. Andrew refused.

This information from the waiter changed the direction of the inquiry team. It seemed likely, from what Andrew had said, that David Wynne Roberts would have been quite capable of committing the murder, but what was not clear was whether or not Bronwen knew that Andrew and David Wynne Roberts were staying together, and, if she did, whether or not she would have approved.

Andrew was clearly frightened of David Wynne Roberts and, during one of their rows, he had threatened to tell Mrs Nixon about their relationship, which might have cost Andrew his job. David Wynne Roberts had said to Andrew that they should form a staff union; he resented the way, in his opinion, the staff were treated by the management. Yet was all this a strong enough motive for such a savage crime? After all, was his grudge not against Andrew rather than Bronwen Nixon?

Detective Chief Superintendent Jack Taylor recalls, 'We had no idea where David Wynne Roberts was at this particular time. He'd had a violent past, and we quite clearly needed to speak to him. We were treating him as a possible suspect at this time. Andrew had told us that, ten days before the murder, Roberts had gone to Blackpool. I therefore dispatched a team of officers to visit every guest house in the area in the hope that we might find out where he'd gone.'

Meanwhile, officers back at the incident room began checking into the background of David Wynne Roberts. It emerged that he had several previous convictions, but one stood out above all the rest.

In July 1969, when Roberts was just fourteen, he was found guilty, after a seven-day trial, of stabbing seventy-three-year-old widow, Mrs Sarah Hughes, several times with a bread knife at her bungalow in Four Mile Bridge, Valley, Anglesey.

Sarah Hughes was wealthy. She owned several properties in the area that she rented out. She was described by locals as being an active community member who looked much younger than her age. She was also a meticulous woman with regular habits. She locked all the doors in the house (including her own bedroom) when she retired for the night at 10 p.m. She had a nervous disposition and would never open the door without ascertaining first, who was there.

Sarah Hughes was at school with David Wynne Roberts' grandmother and was quite friendly with his mother. She often visited their home. Roberts' father drew the plans for the bungalow in which she lived.

When the police were called to the murder scene, the bungalow appeared to have been ransacked and an attempt had been made to drive her car from the garage. It was parked across the driveway in reverse gear. It was known that money was missing from the house, including ten one-pound notes, which had been given to the deceased on the day of her death.

David Wynne Roberts, because he was an acquaintance of the deceased, was initially interviewed as part of routine enquiries, and he gave an alibi. However, detectives found a number of discrepancies in his story and, after more interviews, he made a statement admitting to the murder, along with attempting to drive her car away.

He later denied this in court. When he was searched, £10 was found hidden in his anorak and a subsequent search of his room revealed a book that he had hollowed out in order to hide a wallet. In the wallet were the pound notes that had been given to the deceased on the morning of her death.

In his alleged confession, David Wynne Roberts said he called on Mrs Hughes to see if she wanted firewood. The statement said, 'She called me a young imp and said she would tell my mother I was trying to break into her house. I lost my temper. I followed her in. I picked up the knife and struck her.'

There were a number of remarkable similarities between Sarah Hughes' murder and the one in Cumbria. Detective Chief Superintendent Jack Taylor recalls, 'He had killed an elderly lady in her own home. The woman had been attacked with a knife, her house was ransacked and an attempt had been made to drive her car away. So, as a suspect, David Wynne Roberts immediately went to the top of the list.'

David Wynne Roberts was born on 29 October 1954 in Valley, Anglesey. Up until his conviction in July 1969, he was educated locally. He was released in 1976 and had worked, among other things, as an office manager/administrator. Presently he was unemployed.

The police felt that it was more than likely that David Wynne Roberts was now living in London. He had told Andrew he was going to London, but that was all they had to go on, so enquiries initially concentrated on Blackpool.

The Flamingo is a gay club in Blackpool's town centre. Detectives quickly established that David Wynne Roberts had been a frequent visitor and two officers spent several nights there questioning the locals to see if anyone remembered him. In all, over five hundred members were interviewed. One of them, Chris, had been with David Wynne Roberts the night before the murder:

'I'm a regular visitor to the Flamingo Club and on Saturday the 19th January I'd gone there with two friends. I noticed this man whom I'd seen on several occasions. He was looking at me, but I didn't think he was interested. I chatted to my friends until they left around midnight, and then this man came over and asked me if I wanted to dance. He was about thirty, six foot and had an enormous black moustache. He said his name was Wynne. We danced and chatted about the gay scene. He didn't really say very much. I got fed up and said I was leaving. Wynne said he too was fed up and walked out with me. He was wearing a pale-coloured coat and red scarf.'

Chris had his father's car and drove them to the Lords Guest House where David Wynne Roberts was staying. It was about 1 a.m. David Wynne Roberts made coffee in the downstairs lounge and then they both went upstairs to bed: 'Whilst we were in bed, all he wanted to do was hold me, like he was insecure or something. He was quite passive. He gives the impression of being quite butch, but he's not really.'

The following morning, they woke about 9 a.m. Chris recalls, 'I had this funny feeling about Wynne. He was strange, like he was on drugs or something. He had bags under his eyes as though he didn't sleep a lot, a weird look. I wanted to go because I was feeling uneasy with him. I took a shower about 12 noon, and left Wynne my telephone number. He wrote it in his little red book which had lots of names in it. We walked downstairs and I drove home.'

A few hours later, Chris was asleep in front of the fire when the telephone rang. It was David Wynne Roberts. He was surprised he had rung so soon – it was only 4.30 p.m. He wanted to go for a drink that evening, but Chris was too tired. He suggested meeting later in the week, but when Chris phoned the Lords on Thursday evening, David Wynne Roberts had gone.

The police now knew that David Wynne Roberts was in Blackpool, seventy-five miles away from Ambleside, on Sunday, the day of Bronwen Nixon's murder. They also knew that he had been staying at the Lords Guest House. This was the best lead they had so far, and two officers went immediately to interview the owners.

The guest house was owned by Steve, but he was heavily involved in the motor trade, so the day-to-day running of the business was left in the hands of John, the man he lived with.

John was on duty on Friday 17 January when he had received a telephone call from David Wynne Roberts asking for a room. David Wynne Roberts arrived by taxi from the railway station and said that he was expecting some friends from London on Sunday, and they would be staying all week. He said one of his friends was foreign and did not speak very good English.

On the Friday night, David Wynne Roberts told John he was going to Windermere to meet an ex-lover to sort something out. The following morning, Saturday, John saw David Wynne Roberts again around 10.30 a.m. and he told him that the man had his dad with him, and he was not allowed to stay. He said he had slept at the railway station. John remembered that David Wynne Roberts seemed quite depressed about a relationship that had ended (presumably with Andrew) and wanted to talk.

Saturday evening, John and Steve saw David Wynne Roberts at the Flamingo Club. They saw him dancing with someone whom he later brought back to the guest house. This was Chris. John saw Chris leave the following morning.

On Sunday, David Wynne Roberts stayed in the guest house until around 4 p.m. John recalls, 'On Sunday afternoon, we watched the Saturday-night horror movie which we'd video recorded. Roberts put on his glasses to watch it, and he seemed to have cheered up a bit. It was whilst this film was on that he told me he had read the book about Dennis Neilson. His line of conversation was that he felt sorry for the murderers and understood why they did it. After the movie he went to his room and shortly afterwards he went out.'

That evening, Steve and John did not see David Wynne Roberts and thought he might have left without telling them, so, at about 8 p.m. Steve went to look in his room. His belongings were still there, his bags and clothing.

At around midnight, before he went to bed, Steve locked the doors. He did not see David Wynne Roberts that evening. He and John had been sitting in the lounge, which is at the front of the guest house, with the curtains open, and would undoubtedly have seen David Wynne Roberts had he returned.

The following morning, Monday, Steve got up around 8.30 a.m. He went downstairs and saw the keys to Room 8, the room David Wynne Roberts was staying in, on the hall table. He went upstairs and looked inside the room and noticed that all his belongings had gone. The bed did not look like it had been slept in.

Downstairs, Steve found an envelope and inside was the money David Wynne Roberts owed for his stay and with it was a note that said, 'My friends have been unable to come from London so I have decided to go there, thank you for your hospitality.'

Later that morning, John cleaned Room 8. He emptied the ashtray, stripped the bed and replaced the white plastic liner in the rubbish bin. All he found in the room was a beaker on top of the wardrobe.

The police were now even more anxious to find David Wynne Roberts. Clearly the period of time he was absent from his room covered the time of the murder and this, together with his sudden change of plans, made him the prime suspect.

Detective Chief Superintendent Jack Taylor recalls, 'The problem was that we still had no idea where he was and further enquiries came up with nothing. My gut feeling was that he had returned to London as stated in the note he left, but where exactly, was anybody's guess. I decided therefore to contact *Crimewatch UK* and ask whether they would make a special appeal on our behalf. It was late in the day when I rang the production office, and I wasn't sure whether they would be able to help us out. I was desperate and I knew a nationwide appeal was my best chance of finding him.'

In fact, it was the week of transmission when Detective Chief Superintendent Jack Taylor rang the *Crimewatch* office. All the items for the programme had been decided. Cumbria police were requesting a special appeal for a named person to come forward.

Crimewatch only ever appeals for named suspects in the 'Photocall' part of the programme. This is made up of video recordings of bank and building society robberies, together with photographs of individuals who police need to speak to in connection with various crimes. This section of the programme usually consists of four cases and because they have to be carefully researched, they are selected the week *before* transmission.

However, when Detective Chief Superintendent Jack Taylor telephoned the programme, his case was so serious that it was felt that it should be included in that week's programme. A meeting was immediately arranged between the producer and the BBC's lawyers to discuss the implications of broadcasting such an item. It was important to make sure nothing said, or shown, could jeopardize the eventual trial.

Once a suitable form of words was chosen and agreed upon, then an appeal was made at the very beginning of the programme on Thursday 30 January 1986. It simply asked anyone who had seen David Wynne Roberts or knew his whereabouts to ring in. Cumbria police needed to speak to him in connection with the murder of Bronwen Nixon.

The results of this appeal were quite remarkable.

Fiona, a secretary, was at home in Cumbria watching the programme, and as the picture of David Wynne Roberts flashed on to the screen, she recognized him immediately, but could not initially remember where she had seen him before. Then, after she had thought about it for a few minutes, it all suddenly clicked into place, and she rang the police incident room.

On Sunday 19 January, Fiona had been staying with a friend in Lancaster. That evening she was due to get the bus home to Whitehaven at 6.40 p.m. Her friend was a student at one of the colleges and they had spent the weekend together.

She left her friend at around 6 p.m. on Sunday evening to walk the twenty minutes or so to Lancaster bus station. She arrived in plenty of time and waited outside the travel shop for her bus. She was joined initially by a tallish man with blond hair and a woman. Some time later, she was joined by two more women. One was a student and the other was slightly older and had an Irish accent.

While they were all stood at the bus stop, Fiona remembered a man stopping to talk to the woman with the Irish accent: 'He asked the woman if she knew the times of the buses to Ambleside. She didn't and turned to ask us on his behalf. The girl standing beside me said that there was a bus coming and that it went to Ambleside. He then produced a card which appeared to be a rover ticket for bus travel and asked if he could use it. I told him that I didn't think he could. I remember he had an earring in, but the most prominent thing about him was his moustache. It was very striking and made you look at him twice. His eyes were piercing and staring when he looked at you, and they were the type that you don't forget.'

Fiona recalled that when the bus came, the man chatted to the driver about whether or not he could use his ticket. She remembered that he could not and that he had to pay £3 or £3.50. He then sat down next to the woman with the Irish accent: 'The bus went into Ambleside bus station and I saw the man get off. The girl who I'd been talking to at Lancaster bus station also got off, together with a couple of others.'

Police now knew for certain that David Wynne Roberts was in Ambleside shortly after 8 p.m. on the evening of the murder. However, they were somewhat surprised by the events that immediately followed the *Crimewatch* programme.

Detective Chief Superintendent Jack Taylor was sitting in the studio minutes after the programme had finished when a phone call came through from the police station in Chiswick, west London. David Wynne Roberts had been watching *Crimewatch* and seen himself on the television. He had walked straight into Chiswick police station.

He told the duty officer, 'My photograph appeared on *Crimewatch* this evening in connection with the murder of Mrs Nixon in Ambleside. I've come here with my solicitor as I understand you have a few questions to ask me.'

Jack Taylor was amazed that David Wynne Roberts had given himself up: 'I couldn't believe that he'd walked straight in off the street. I now had a problem because I didn't want to start interviewing him in London, when most of my officers and all the investigation had taken place in Cumbria. So I despatched two officers who had come to London with me to Chiswick, and they drove Roberts through the night back to Kendal police station.'

On 1 January 1986, the Police and Criminal Evidence Act (PACE) had come into force in England and Wales, and part of the procedures prescribed in the Act is that interviews are timed, that is, once a person is detained for a particular offence, the minute he starts to be questioned about that offence, the clock is turned on. So, no questions were put to David Wynne Roberts at Chiswick, or indeed at any time during the drive north.

Under PACE, the police are only allowed to hold a suspect for an initial twenty-four-hour period without bringing charges. After this time, an extension has to be applied for, initially from the superintendent and then from a magistrates' court at a full hearing, held in private, at which the suspect is entitled to be both present and legally represented. Moreover, there is no power to hold anyone for more than twenty-four hours unless he is suspected of having committed a grave offence. The maximum amount of time the magistrates can authorize a suspect to be detained without being charged is ninety-six hours.

Before PACE came into force, the police were guided by Judge's Rules, which were loosely written and open to misinterpretation. Very often it was down to the discretion of the arresting officer as to how a suspect was treated. Although it was written that a suspect had the right to a solicitor, this was sometimes interpreted differently and access was denied. It was therefore accepted that a thorough review of the criminal procedures covering the time from arrest through to trial was needed.

In 1978 the Royal Commission on Criminal Procedure was established to do this. Its aim was to establish a proper balance between the interests of the community as a whole in seeing offenders brought before the courts and the rights of individuals suspected of offences. The Government introduced the Police and Criminal Evidence Bill to the House in November 1982. It received its royal assent in October 1984, and the majority of its provisions came into force on 1 January 1986.

As a result, the police now have strong rules to adhere to once a person has been arrested. Suspects are initially read their rights and told that they have a right to a solicitor. A custody record must be opened as soon as someone is brought into the police station under arrest. This is a written summary of the individual's movements – when they were detained, and if they needed to be transferred to another station, the time and details must be recorded; likewise if they are taken before a court.

All interviews between the offender and police officers must be recorded. Breaks from interviewing are made at recognized meal times and short breaks for refreshment will also be provided at intervals of approximately two hours.

A person under arrest also has the right to request that someone, usually family, be told and notified of their arrest at public expense. They may also receive visits at the custody officer's discretion, and are allowed to speak on the telephone for a reasonable time to one person, although they must be told that this will be listened to and may be used in evidence.

So, Detective Chief Superintendent Jack Taylor and his team not only had the job of investigating a murder, they had the added complication of dealing with a whole new body of legislation that, if breached, could jeopardize the inquiry. He remembers, 'We really were just feeling our way with PACE. I'd been on a one-day course, like most other officers, but I felt I needed all the help I could get. The last thing I wanted was to make a mistake and risk losing the case on some technicality.'

Detective Chief Superintendent Jack Taylor therefore involved the Crown Prosecution Service, who are responsible for preparing criminal cases for court, at a very early stage. He made frequent visits to London, keeping them informed of his every move.

The morning after *Crimewatch*, Detective Chief Superintendent Jack Taylor had flown back to Cumbria and he held a briefing in the library at Kendal police station: 'Now there is no doubt in my mind that this is our man. I want to talk about strategy – how we approach this first interview. It seems fairly obvious to me that a man who walks into a police station with a solicitor is going to be prepared to stick it out. So, I don't think under the circumstances that he is going to admit this. The way to approach it is to try and find out exactly where he's been since he left Rothay Manor. Let's break down his alibi and see where we go from there. Approach it nice and gently at this stage, don't drop the previous murder on him at this stage, I want to keep it for later.'

Two officers began interviewing David Wynne Roberts at 3.20 p.m. He appeared calm and relaxed. The police officer began:

'*On Sunday 19 January, Mrs Nixon, hotelier of the Rothay Manor Hotel, was murdered. I believe you knew her?*'
'*I met her once or twice.*'
'*We first of all wish to know some of your movements over the period from November last year until yesterday.*'
'*I came to Blackpool in November and was staying in a guest house on South Shore. I was signing on at the DHSS in Blackpool. I met Andrew from the Rothay Manor on December 9th at a disco. That evening we drove back to Ambleside and I stayed there for about ten days. I returned to Blackpool to sign on. Then I got the train back to Oxenholme where Andrew met me and I stayed with him for about a week. Then we went to Blackpool. This carried on for about eleven weeks, some weekends we stayed in Blackpool and others we spent in Ambleside.*'

David Wynne Roberts said that they sometimes travelled by train, other times they used Andrew's car. He said he never caught the bus. He said the last time he was in Ambleside was between Monday 6 January – the night of the Rothay Manor staff party – and Thursday 9 January. He had seen Andrew on 17 January, but this was in Kendal, and he had spent the weekend in Blackpool at the Lords Guest House.

David Wynne Roberts went through the events of that weekend, the weekend of the murder. Everything that he told the police officers fitted in with what other witnesses had said: he arrived at the Lords on Friday afternoon and rang Andrew. They met that evening in Kendal. David Wynne Roberts was going to stay at a guest house in Kendal, but the owners were out. He slept on the railway station and returned to Blackpool the next morning. Saturday evening, he went to the Flamingo Club and met a man called Chris. They spent the night together. Sunday around 4 p.m. he rang Chris to ask him if he wanted to go out.

However, from this point onwards, David Wynne Roberts' version of events on Sunday evening differed from the police's belief of what actually happened. David Wynne Roberts said he had a shower around 5 p.m. and then went to a snack bar. He had fallen asleep in his room until about 8 p.m. and had then gone to the Flamingo Club until around 11.30 p.m. He spent the night back at the Lords and left for London the following morning. He had a sandwich at the railway station about 7.30 a.m. and caught the 7.50 train to London. He phoned a friend in London, whilst changing trains in Preston, to tell him what time he was arriving. The friend was called Renato. Finally police asked him:

'Between 4 p.m. on Sunday 19 January and 8 a.m. on Monday 20 January did you leave Blackpool at all?'
'No.'

At this point, the interview was halted. It was 4.53 p.m. David Wynne Roberts was sticking to his story, and police now needed to check the details of what he had told them.

Meanwhile, the two detectives who had interviewed

Steve and John at the Lords Guest House in Blackpool had a stroke of luck.

The council had failed to collect the rubbish from the guest house on the due day because it was not left in the right place. It was just possible that David Wynne Roberts had thrown something away of vital importance. Police took three huge sacks to a large garage and began searching through their contents.

Several hours later, at the bottom of one of these large sacks, they found the corners of two black cards bearing the name 'NIXON' in gold lettering. Along with these cards was a tightly rolled ball of newspaper. It was an advert from the *Observer* newspaper for the Royal Festival Ballet, and the *Nutcracker* was marked with two red crosses. A telephone number was written on the advertisement in black biro. Also in the bottom of the bag were eight torn fragments of a buff-coloured card that appeared to bear the name Rothay Manor, and a letter that was signed 'Wynne'.

This was indeed extremely useful, but at this stage it did not directly link David Wynne Roberts with Mrs Nixon's murder because it was quite possible that he had got these during the time he was staying with Andrew.

As a matter of course, the cards were shown to Stephen Nixon who confirmed that they were his mother's old business cards. He also confirmed that the writing on the scrap of newspaper was his mother's but, more importantly, he told police that these papers would very likely have been in his mother's purse. If this was the case, what was David Roberts doing with Mrs Nixon's purse and how had he acquired it?

A detective made enquiries at the Royal Festival Hall booking office and discovered that the number written in biro on the advertisement was for the credit card line. He was given a computer readout that showed that Bronwen Nixon had paid for two tickets for the

Nutcracker by credit card and, more crucially, it gave the booking time as exactly 6 p.m. on 9 January.

This then proved that David Wynne Roberts had been at the Rothay Manor Hotel some time after 6 p.m. on Thursday 9 January. Furthermore, it was likely that Bronwen had kept these papers in her purse and the only way David Wynne Roberts could have got them was if he had gone into her cottage.

The police also found among the rubbish sheddings of red cashmere fibres, the size of two tiny pills. The forensic scientist explained, 'When we looked at the red fibres in conjunction with the samples we'd taken from the murder scene, and the car, we found they were all similar. This suggested that the same person who had been at the murder scene had also been in the car, and subsequently at the Lords Guest House.'

Meanwhile, officers back at Kendal police station continued interviewing David Wynne Roberts:

'What did you think when you saw and heard you were on Crimewatch?'
'My first thought was that Andrew had informed the police that I'd been staying with him and that they wanted to question me on why I was there.'
'Are you quite sure of the account that you have given us of your movements on Sunday 19th/Monday 20th of January is correct?'
'All the information I have given is correct.'
'That is not what I believe – you left the Lords Guest House at 4 p.m. on Sunday. You were not seen again by anyone at the hotel. Is that right?'
'The time is probably accurate, but I did return to the hotel.' (Wynne Roberts had also told the police that he had met a man called Brian at the Flamingo on Sunday night. This too turned out to be incorrect.)
'You didn't meet Brian at the Flamingo Club on Sunday night. He saw you there the previous night. Is that correct?'

'He was there on the Saturday and Sunday.'
'At 6.40 p.m. that Sunday night you caught a bus at Lancaster and travelled to Ambleside. Is that correct?'
'No.'
'You were seen to get off the bus in Ambleside at about 8.15 p.m. on Sunday night. Is that correct?'
'No.'
'You say you were in the Lords in Blackpool at 11.45 p.m. and went straight to your room. Is that correct?'
'Yes.'
'The owner of the hotel checked your room at midnight on Sunday the 19th and you were not in the room. What do you say to that?'
'If he did check it then it must have been at a different time.'
'Why are you telling lies, Mr Roberts?'
'I am not telling lies.'

A few days after *Crimewatch* the woman with the Irish accent, whom Fiona had seen sitting next to David Wynne Roberts on the bus, came forward. She had seen details of the case in the local newspapers.

It turned out that she lived in Kendal and because her sister had suffered a stroke at the beginning of January, she visited her most weekends in Blackpool. On Sunday evening, 19 January, she got a bus from Bispham to Blackpool, arriving in Blackpool depot at about 4 p.m. She then had to wait for about an hour for her connection from Blackpool to Lancaster. It was a cold evening and she saw her bus arrive about ten minutes early so she approached the driver and asked him if she could get on. He agreed. She had only been on the bus for about five minutes when she saw a man get on: 'He was about thirty, thinly built with dark collar-length hair. He had a large, bushy moustache. He appeared not to have shaven for a couple of days. I overheard him talking to the driver about going to Ambleside. This man then went upstairs. I didn't see him again until we both got off the bus at Lancaster some time after 6 p.m. A couple of minutes later, this man approached me. He asked me which bus I was waiting for and whether it went to Ambleside. I couldn't tell him for sure if it did and a general discussion took place between two other girls, who were also waiting for the bus, about this man's bus to Ambleside.'

The woman remembered that the bus was about fifteen minutes late. The man spoke to the driver about his ticket, which was not valid, and he had to pay extra to get to Ambleside. When he walked on to the bus, he approached her and said, 'I'll join you.'

She remembers, 'I thought it was a bit funny as there were other seats empty. We spoke a little during the journey. He said he was on holiday and I thought it a bit queer for this time of year. As the bus was running a bit late, he seemed to be agitated, as if he was wanting to get to Ambleside in a hurry. We arrived in Kendal about 8 p.m. and as far as I can remember I was the only person to get off. This was the last time I saw him. He said "Take care" as I got off. When I heard about the death of Bronwen Nixon and saw a picture of this man in the paper, I recognized him as the same man I had travelled with.'

The police now had several witnesses who claimed to have seen David Wynne Roberts on the bus on Sunday 19 January. Roberts was still denying leaving Blackpool, so they decided to hold an identification parade. David Wynne Roberts refused on the basis that his photograph had been shown both on television and in the press.

However, under PACE, if a suspect refuses to take part in an identification parade, then a 'confrontation' can be arranged between the witnesses and the offender. David Wynne Roberts had several choices. The first was the usual parade, where he would line up with at least eight others who were similar in appearance to him. The second was to allow the witnesses to see him in a group of people. Both of these he refused. So, finally, it had to be arranged for David Wynne Roberts to sit on his own behind a one-way mirror and be confronted by the witnesses. Unfortunately, Cumbria Police did not have a suitable mirror at that time so they borrowed one from the Strathclyde police in Glasgow.

In order to arrange for all the witnesses to confront David Wynne Roberts, the police needed more time. They had already been granted several time extensions by the magistrates' court and this was going to be their last chance to keep him in custody. Unfortunately it was Sunday, and the courts are closed on Sunday so a special court was set up in the magistrates' clerk's office, a prefabricated building next to the police station.

Detective Chief Superintendent Jack Taylor explained to the court that David Wynne Roberts was going to be seen by several witnesses who might identify him, after which he would either be released or charged. After a short hearing, the police were granted a further thirty-six hours. Jack Taylor recalls, 'From a police point of view, going to the magistrates' court with the suspect is very unfair. It allows the defendant to know the exact situation the inquiry has reached. We had to keep David Wynne Roberts because after the initial interview he refused to answer any more questions and we had a number of outstanding witnesses to approach. He also had a previous conviction for murder in similar circumstances and, in my opinion, his release would have further frustrated the inquiry.'

During his interview, David Wynne Roberts had given police the name of his Maltese friend, Renato, whom he had stayed with in London. Two officers went immediately to visit him.

Renato had met David Wynne Roberts in late December 1984 in a gay club in London. They had kept in touch through letters and phone calls ever since. On Monday 13 January, he had arrived at Heathrow airport and David Wynne Roberts had met him. They had then spent several days together and, on Friday 17 January, David Wynne Roberts told Renato that he was going to Blackpool; 'He already had a ticket and said that it was too expensive to live in London. I didn't expect to see him again during my holiday. He told me he was going to stay in the Lords Guest House, and he wanted me to go with him, but I said no. At about 3 a.m. on either Saturday or Sunday morning, the 18/19 January, he telephoned me. He said he was all wet, and outside in the middle of nowhere. He mentioned the name Kendal. He gave no indication that he was coming back to London. I next heard from him at 8 a.m. on Monday 20 January. He told me he was returning to London and asked would I meet him at Euston.'

They spent several more nights together before Renato went to visit an uncle in Bristol on 30 January. He recalled that they had exchanged several items of clothing: 'I exchanged my black and white scarf with Wynne for a red one that he was already wearing. He said it irritated his neck. He'd bought it in Harrods last year for £25. He gave me his beige shoes and a pair of boots. He said his feet were cold when he wore them. He also gave me a pair of black leather gloves and a grey wallet. He said the gloves had belonged to his friend, Andrew, from Kendal. Wynne said that he couldn't grip with them and that I could have them. He said he'd washed them. I can't remember when exactly he gave them to me, but it was some time after he'd returned from Blackpool on the 20th of January. The wallet wasn't the type I would use, but I kept it and thought maybe I'd give it to my sister.'

Detectives could not believe what they had found. They now had a red cashmere scarf that had belonged to David Wynne Roberts in their possession. If the fibres matched those discovered on Bronwen's body, and in her car, then they had the strongest evidence yet against David Wynne Roberts.

It was an enormous stroke of luck that David Wynne Roberts had told them about Renato. Indeed, he was the only person, apart from Andrew, that David Wynne Roberts gave any details about, and the very next day Renato was due to fly back to Malta. He would very likely have taken the scarf with him, so the police would never have found it.

The same day as police in London had spoken to Renato, the confrontation between David Wynne Roberts and several witnesses took place at Kendal. Those called included the man who had seen David Wynne Roberts driving the blue Honda on Monday morning 20 January and Fiona, who had seen David Wynne Roberts get off the bus at Ambleside on the Sunday evening.

When the witnesses walked into the room, David Wynne Roberts was sitting behind a mirror. He could not see them, but he was quite capable of hearing everything that was said. Four out of five people positively identified him.

When further questions were put to David Wynne Roberts, he refused to answer any of them.

Forensic experts had meanwhile examined the red scarf and fibres taken from it matched precisely, in colour and in microscopic appearance, those already found with the body, in the car and in the rubbish.

Detective Chief Superintendent Jack Taylor summed up his feelings: 'If the scarf had gone back to Malta we may never have found it, and if we hadn't found it then it is extremely unlikely that we would ever have proved this case. We now had enough evidence to link Roberts to the murder and so, on February 3rd, three days after the *Crimewatch* programme, he was charged with Bronwen Nixon's murder.'

David Wynne Roberts pleaded not guilty in court and therefore the motive for the murder will never really be known. There were certainly a number of similarities between this murder and the previous murder he had committed. The motive could have been robbery, but the crime seemed very violent for this. Was it that David Wynne Roberts blamed Bronwen Nixon for the break up of his relationship with Andrew (Andrew had used Bronwen's disapproval of Wynne sharing his room as an excuse to end the affair) or was it that he had some other grudge against her that has never been revealed?

At Manchester Crown Court on 1 December 1986, Roberts was found guilty and sentenced to life imprisonment.

Detective Chief Superintendent Jack Taylor recalls, 'It certainly was an interesting case to work on. We average about ten murders a year in Cumbria, and this is one that stands out from the rest, not least because of the new legislation which was such an integral part of it. The response from *Crimewatch* was quite incredible and this, combined with dogged police work, really paid off.'

David Wynne Roberts has continued to deny his involvement in this crime.

3

BIRKENHEAD
SERIAL RAPIST

DNA fingerprinting has become crucial in linking an individual with a crime. Leave a hair root, a drop of blood, a trace of semen or some saliva and you have left a calling card because every living cell contains a DNA pattern unique to its owner. When this is analysed, it can be read like a supermarket bar code and enables police to identify someone with a greater deal of certainty.

In court, the prosecution has come to rely on this revolutionary technique, but what happens when the criminal has left no DNA evidence, in fact, no forensic evidence at all? This was the situation facing the Merseyside police in a series of rape cases in 1990 and 1991.

Detective Sergeant Frank Anderson had worked in the Criminal Investigation Department for about sixteen years and, for the past four years, he had been based at Birkenhead police station. Birkenhead is one of the busiest stations in the Wirral division, with the highest number of reported crimes in the whole of Merseyside.

Birkenhead, with a population of 280 000 people, is situated on the west bank of the River Mersey. There are few jobs – unemployment is well above the national average – and the famous shipbuilders, Laird, closed down in the summer of 1993. William Laird began his company back in 1825 and famous ships like *The Alabama* and *Ark Royal* were built in Birkenhead.

Shipbuilding has been one of the mainstays of the town, but, sadly, much of this has now gone.

Not far from the docks is a park about 200 yards square. It is surrounded by houses and locally is called 'the Rec'. It is frequently used by children and backs on to Tollemache Road, the main road through Birkenhead.

On Thursday 8 November 1990 at about midnight, the police received an urgent call from a man who lived near 'the Rec'. He said his wife had been walking home across the park about an hour or so ago, when she was attacked and raped. A policewoman went to see her immediately.

In order to protect the identities of all the victims, none of their real names has been used in the relating of this case. We will call the first victim Jane.

Jane was taken to the police station to the rape suite where she was interviewed and examined. Naturally, she was very distressed and upset by what had happened; her whole body was shaking. She said a man had attacked her from behind and raped her as she was walking home. She had never seen him before.

The following morning, Detective Sergeant Frank Anderson came on duty and, as always, looked through the night reports to see what had happened. He immediately saw the rape allegation and his attention was drawn to the victim – Jane; he had known her for about sixteen years.

Jane was thirty-two and had lived in Birkenhead all her life. She had previous convictions for possession of drugs and shoplifting. Sergeant Anderson remembers, 'I was very surprised to see Jane's name on the crime report. I went round to her house immediately to check out details of her statement and see how she was coping. Jane came from a good, middle-class background, but in her late teens she'd associated with a crowd who'd dabbled in drugs. She became a regular user and was stealing to feed her habit. This apart, she was very respectable and took pride in her appearance.'

Jane lived with her husband in a rented house not far from the Rec. She was able to give Detective Sergeant Frank Anderson a very detailed description of her attacker and he took her to Merseyside Police Headquarters in Liverpool where she compiled an E Fit of the rapist.

An E Fit is a picture of a face that is built up by the use of computer graphics. The victim, while sitting beside the graphic artist, compiles an image that is as near a likeness to the suspect as she can remember. This technique has proved very successful and many police forces prefer this method to the old Photofit because it produces a much more life-like impression, so when it is published there is a greater chance of someone recognizing the face.

For Merseyside police, this was all they had to go on. The forensic reports revealed nothing and once press reports had died down and house-to-house enquiries were exhausted, the investigation soon ground to a halt. Officers, fearing he might strike again, had even driven around the area at night looking for him, but had found nothing.

Then, five months later, on Thursday 4 April 1991, another rape was reported. A fifteen-year-old schoolgirl, Angela, was walking home in the early hours after she had had a row with her parents, when she was attacked.

Angela had been aware of a shadow behind her as she walked along: 'I did not turn round at that point but got to the junction when I was grabbed around my mouth from behind by a person using their left hand. My right arm was held down. I was screaming. He pushed me into some bushes. The man put his hand tighter over my mouth and told me to keep quiet. We walked through some trees and once out of them I could see Bidston Observatory. He took my jacket off me and dropped it to the floor. He then got hold of my jumper and shirt and tried to pull them over my head.'

A few minutes later he raped her. After the attack, he gave her a lift to a pub yards from her home. As soon as she got inside her home she told her mother who rang the police. A policewoman went straight to her house and she was taken into Birkenhead police station to the rape suite where she was examined.

The next morning, Detective Sergeant Frank Anderson came on duty and looked through the nightly crime reports: 'It's a very busy police station and sometimes when you come on duty you have half a dozen prisoners in the cells to deal with, plus about twenty reported crimes which have come in overnight. However, when I read the details of this rape, something just clicked. I think it was the description of the attack that made me think immediately of Jane's attack five months earlier. It was so similar and I began to make enquiries straight away.'

This time, the attack had happened on Bidstone Hill, a well-known beauty spot near to the Bidstone Observatory. It is about half a mile from the Rec on the other side of Tollemache Road.

Angela recalled that the man said his name was Terry, he had short dark hair and was about forty years old. He was clean and tidy and spoke quietly with a Birkenhead accent.

Detective Sergeant Frank Anderson went to visit Angela after the attack and was surprised at how well she was coping with her ordeal: 'She looked much older than fifteen and was pretty streetwise. She was very open about what had happened. She'd accepted it and wasn't going to let it get her down. She was desperate for him to be caught, and gave us a very detailed description.'

However, before detectives had time to follow up these details, another attack was reported. It happened the day after the rape, Friday 5 April at 11.30 p.m. Claire, an art student, lived with her boyfriend in a house overlooking the Rec: 'I'd been in the house all evening, listening to music and watching the television, generally just passing time waiting for my boyfriend to come home. At about 11.15 p.m., I got bored so decided to go for a walk. I got my Walkman and started listening to Irish music. I'd borrowed the tape from a friend. I was walking in the Rec close to the swings when I felt someone grab me. The man put his hand over my mouth.'

Claire was subjected to a very serious indecent assault. She met her boyfriend moments after her attacker left and together they telephoned the police. Claire described the man as white, clean-shaven and about forty years old.

The police were now very concerned that they had a serial sex attacker on the streets of Birkenhead. A major investigation was launched, headed by Detective Chief Inspector Chris Kemp, deputy head of CID for the Wirral area. He had first worked in Wallasey as a sergeant twenty years ago. Born in Durham, he had spent a number of years working in Yorkshire, where he began his training in the police cadets. He was the ideal man to run the Birkenhead rape inquiry because part of his job was to train officers on the Holmes computer.

The Home Office Large Major Enquiry System (Holmes) is used by all forces investigating major crimes and is a database system that first came into operation in January 1986. It enables the investigating team to enter, store, relate, retrieve and output documents essential to the inquiry. These include statements, messages, house-to-house questionnaires and officers' reports. The future actions of the officers can also be stored, along with addresses, telephone numbers and sequences of events.

Every force in the UK operates at least one Holmes system and the central processor and terminals are usually located at a force's headquarters. These can be moved to wherever necessary once an investigation begins. The office manager is then in charge of making sure all relevant information is loaded into the system.

Officers go on a four-week training course before using the equipment. The Holmes system is now essential to any major inquiry.

Detective Chief Inspector Kemp's first briefing was of a team of around forty officers: 'Between Thursday 8 November 1990 and Sunday 14 April 1991, there has been a series of rapes and indecent assaults around Birkenhead Park, and for a number of reasons I think we are looking at one man: the descriptions of the offender are virtually the same in every case – forty years old, five feet nine inches tall and stockily built with short, dark brown hair. He had a greyish, white car and on more than one occasion was wearing a black leather jacket and jeans. In every case, the method of attack was the same. His initial approach was always from behind and he used part of the victim's clothing to restrict their movement. I feel because of the detailed knowledge he has of the parks and pathways around Birkenhead, we must be looking for a local man.'

Over the next week or so, two more indecent assaults were reported in the same area, but this time the victims managed to struggle free.

Detective Chief Inspector Chris Kemp had upwards of fifty officers working for him and it was one of the biggest investigations ever mounted by Merseyside Police. Female officers specially trained in counselling rape victims were brought in alongside a team of uniformed officers from the operational support division who had expertise in house-to-house enquiries. It was a densely populated area and there were around a thousand houses to visit.

However, the investigation team was faced with a number of immediate problems. They had no forensic evidence whatsoever. In each case, the rapist never ejaculated and he did not leave anything at the scene of the crime. There were no independent witnesses to any of the attacks. The victims would have to give evidence in court and, because of some of their lifestyles – walking the streets at night, drug dependent with previous convictions – it would be easy for the defence to tear their story apart, making them lose all credibility in the witness box.

A recent Home Office study shows that cases of attempted rape and rape have only a one in four chance of resulting in a conviction. Many cases are dropped before they get to court, either because the police feel there is insufficient evidence or because the woman herself decides against testifying in court. Very often, if the case does reach court, the assailant is acquitted or the case dropped because of lack of evidence. It is difficult in rape cases to get corroborative evidence and, even if DNA evidence is found, the rapist can argue that the event occurred with the woman's consent.

Detective Chief Inspector Chris Kemp knew that it was going to be a very hard case to solve: 'We recognized that if we were going to get anywhere with this, then we had to prove a combination of offences to get credibility. This is because if you take each one separately and you only prosecute on that particular case, then the character of the complainant becomes a critical factor and it would be unlikely that we would have prosecuted any single one to conviction. We brought in the Crown Prosecution Service, who are responsible for preparing criminal cases for court, at a very early stage and went through everything with them.'

Detective Sergeant Frank Anderson's main task was to collate the information as it came in and then try to build up some kind of picture of the man they were looking for: 'I spent an awful lot of time with the victims, going over their stories, making sure we'd missed nothing. We had a very serious sex offender on our hands and I thought it possible that he might kill his next victim. I drove round Birkenhead in my car, taking the routes he must have taken, wondering what sort of person he was. Did he live alone? Did he live in the area? Did he have friends? Maybe he was a family man? Somehow or other I was determined to catch him.'

The one major clue detectives had to work with was the picture they had of the face of the offender. They already had the E Fit put together with the help of Jane, and the schoolgirl, Angela, had managed to piece together an artist's impression of her attacker, while Claire, the art student, had actually drawn a portrait of her assailant herself. The similarities between all the images were quite remarkable, and this gave the investigation team an enormous boost. Detective Sergeant Frank Anderson remembers: 'It was incredible that three victims had independently given us almost identical impressions of the man and, to make the case even stronger, Claire had actually drawn her own picture of the rapist. We now had a really positive lead and decided to print the picture in the local press to see if anyone recognized him.'

The initial response was quite good. A number of women came forward, saying that they had been attacked by this man and were anxious to give as much information as possible. However, several victims were prostitutes, and when they realized that they would have to go to court to give evidence, they decided not to proceed with their allegations.

For Detective Chief Inspector Chris Kemp and his team it was a very frustrating time: 'Here were a number of potential victims who would undoubtedly have strengthened our case, but for reasons of their own they decided not to pursue their allegations. In tandem with these press releases I was running the house-to-house enquiries. After a few weeks, we had really stormed the area and got virtually nowhere. Throughout April we worked extremely hard, but got no leads of any value whatsoever. It was at this point that I went to our headquarters and suggested we contact *Crimewatch UK*. We were desperate to widen the appeal and get national coverage.'

It was towards the end of May when Detective Sergeant Frank Anderson telephoned the *Crimewatch* office. The police had little to go on, except a Photofit of the offender, so there was not enough information for a filmed reconstruction. Instead, it was decided to put the case into the 'incident desk' slot. This is made up of around four cases each month, presented by two police officers, Superintendent David Hatcher and Detective Constable Jacqui Hames. The incident desk part of the programme gives details of cases where information is thin on the ground and detectives are desperate for a short national appeal that might boost the inquiry.

On 13 June 1991, the item was broadcast, and the Photofit of the rapist, together with a map of the area, formed the basis of the appeal.

A large number of calls came into the studio that night. Most suggested different names for the artist's impression. *Crimewatch* had (up until 1992) forty lines into the studio. Twenty calls were answered immediately by detectives and programme researchers, while the other twenty were directed to an answerphone. It is a complicated system and there is only one studio in the whole of Television Centre geared up to deal with it. Despite all these phone lines, it was apparent that a large number of callers failed to get through, so, in 1993, at a cost of several thousand pounds, another eight lines were installed. A freephone number was also introduced, and the programme now receives a total of around two thousand calls each month. In addition, police incident room numbers are given out and, depending on the individual cases, they too can take many hundreds more calls.

After the appeal for information about the Birkenhead rapist went out, one call really excited detectives. It came from a local taxi driver who said he recognized the man in the Photofit: 'I'm a hackney cab driver and about eighteen months ago I was parked outside Rupert's Club in Birkenhead. It was about 3 a.m. Next to me was parked a white Maxi. The driver was about forty with short hair and I thought he was pirating [looking for illegal trade as there is a taxi rank in the road], so I took a good look at him and made a note of his car number. After about half an hour, he drove off and I followed him. I later saw his car parked and he was walking along. Close by him was a girl I knew as Karen. He appeared to be making his way towards her, but when he saw me, he turned back. I shouted across to Karen and told her that I thought she was being followed. I told her to make her way to the taxi rank in Argyle Street. As I drove round the corner, I saw a police car, so I stopped and told them what had happened. They spoke to the man, and then he drove off.'

The taxi driver also said that he had seen this man about twenty times since then and he was usually in the Tollemache Road area of Birkenhead. He was either walking or in his white Maxi car.

This, of course, was a major breakthrough for the police. It seemed that the taxi driver had described the man they were looking for precisely. He even had details of the car, which the police had not previously revealed, but unfortunately he had no idea where the man lived, what his name was or, indeed, any further information to help them find him.

Detective Sergeant Frank Anderson described the mood of the inquiry team: 'We were so elated after *Crimewatch*. This was our first positive lead on the suspect; we felt sure the man the taxi driver had described was our man, but we had no idea where he was now. The mood changed from a big high to a big low. We were just going to have to bide our time until we got the break we so desperately needed. It was at this point that I felt him begin to slip through our fingers.'

It was indeed to prove a frustrating time for the

police because on several occasions they were within minutes of catching him, but when they got to the scene, he had vanished.

Two of the victims, Angela and Claire, had become friends since meeting each other in the police station after compiling their artist's impressions. Angela recalls, 'We both talked at length about our attacks and the offender. We felt better talking together because we could understand how each other felt.'

The two girls sometimes went out walking and one day, as they were going along Tollemache Road, they thought they saw him. Angela remembers, 'Since my attack I have been keeping a look out for his car. We were walking along when this car drew up almost level with me. It was identical to the one the rapist had. I looked at the driver and stopped. We were almost opposite the Rec. The window on the driver's side was closed, but I could still see him. It was the same man who had raped me. I could only see the side of his face but it was definitely him. He didn't see me. I shouted to Claire, "That's him in the car that's just driven past. Ring the police."'

Unfortunately, by the time the police arrived, the man had gone.

Then, six weeks after the *Crimewatch* programme, on Sunday morning, 28 July at around 6 a.m. the taxi driver was again driving through Birkenhead. He stopped at a set of traffic lights, looked across towards the pavement and saw the man he had recognized from the *Crimewatch* Photofit walking towards him: 'He was wearing a blue shell suit with a red and white flash on the jacket. Just as I saw him, I saw Karen as well. I stopped and shouted to Karen that I thought she was being followed. I went straight to the police station and told them what I'd seen. Then, when I left the station I picked up a fare and was driving along when I saw the man again. Only this time, he was in a dark brown

Volvo, heading towards the town centre. I made a note of the registration number and telephoned the police.'

The Volvo's registration number was circulated to all patrol cars in the Wirral area, and it took just five minutes for one of them to find it. The car was by the entrance to the park on Park Road East, Birkenhead, and the driver was inside reading a newspaper. Officers thought he looked remarkably like the Photofit picture of the rapist. When they asked him what he was doing, he said he had been to the toilet, then the bank and had just bought a paper. They were not satisfied with the answers so they arrested him and took him to Birkenhead police station.

Detective Chief Inspector Chris Kemp had taken the weekend off and Detective Sergeant Frank Anderson was at home off duty. He was fast asleep when the telephone rang: 'I couldn't believe it when the officer told me they'd nicked him. I was so excited I couldn't get dressed quickly enough. I sent two officers to try to find the girl he'd been following because I thought she might have crucial information. I was desperate to meet the man and see for myself what he was like. I couldn't wait to get to work.'

When Detective Sergeant Frank Anderson arrived at the station, he met up with a team of officers to discuss the strategy of the day. They knew it was unlikely that the suspect would admit to any of the allegations because of the serious nature of the crimes. What they needed to get was as much background information from him as possible. Where he worked, how he spent his time. Details of his arrest were circulated to all other forces outside the area in case further offences against him were being investigated.

Two officers went round to the suspect's house to explain to his wife what was happening and then, before Detective Sergeant Anderson started the interview, he went through all the statements of the complainants once more to refresh his memory.

The senior officer on duty that weekend, Detective Chief Inspector Williams, went with Detective Sergeant Frank Anderson into the interview room. Frank Anderson recalls, 'It was about 12 o'clock when we walked into the room. I was surprised how respectable the man looked. He was clean-shaven and well dressed. He appeared very calm as I began by asking him his name:

'Paul Leslie Richard Spencer, born on the 18th of March 1954.'

'First of all, Paul, do you know why you've been arrested?'

'On suspicion of being involved with the rapes in Birkenhead.'

'That's correct. And you have spoken to your solicitor?'

'Yes.'

'Can you tell me a little about yourself, Paul?'

'I've lived with my common law wife for thirteen years and we have five children. I've lived at my present address for eight years and have been employed as the manager of a bowling centre for five years. I work shifts, sometimes I start at 9.30 a.m. and finish about 6 p.m. Other times I start at 4 p.m. and go on till around midnight ... but if we're busy then we stay open later and it can be between 1.30 and 2 a.m. when I leave.'

'OK, as we've already stated you've been arrested on suspicion of rape, now you are aware of the rapes that have occurred in Birkenhead?'

'Yes.'

'Can I just ask you now, are you responsible for these series of rapes?'

'No.'

Detective Sergeant Frank Anderson was surprised by how cool the man remained. He never raised his voice or lost his temper, even when accused of the crimes.

'What car do you own?'
'A Volvo 244 saloon with a brown interior.'
'How long have you had that car?'
'Since January.'
'What car did you have prior to that?'
'An Austin Maxi.'
'What colour was that?'
'White.'

Despite his calm exterior Detective Sergeant Frank Anderson could detect the occasional dryness in the man's mouth, suggesting a hidden nervousness. He asked him why he was up so early that morning:

'I got up early because I'd got a budget business plan to produce for a managers' meeting on Friday. I've just been promoted and I've taken the reins of the business. I needed some figures, so I went back to the bowl.'
'What time would that be?'
'About 5 a.m.'
'Isn't that unusual?'
'Yes, but I needed the figures.'

He then went on to explain that he often worked in the car to get some peace and quiet. That is what he was doing this morning. He had been to the bowling centre, collected the figures and was going to do some work in the car before going home to get changed. He was then going to drive back to work for 8.30 a.m.

Detective Sergeant Frank Anderson remembers thinking, 'His story just didn't add up. He was due to start work at 8.30, and he claimed to be incredibly busy. So why did he waste so much time driving back and forth, walking round Birkenhead town centre in the early hours of the morning, then sitting in his car reading the newspaper? It just wasn't a logical explanation. It would have been far easier for him to have gone into work an hour or so earlier.'

The police officers went over the morning's events with Mr Spencer several times, questioning the details, but throughout, his story remained the same. They then went on to question him about his visit to the bank that morning:

'How much money did you have on you this morning?'
'Altogether I had about £13.'
'You had enough money for the rest of the day. You didn't need any more did you?'
'No.'
'So why did you tell the police officers you'd been to the bank?'
'I think it was just panic.'
'Panic? Panic over what? You'd done nothing wrong. You know you're a businessman and you'd been to the bowl to pick up some documentation and you're sitting around like an innocent member of the public reading your paper.'
'Yes, well I just said I'd been to the bank.'
'Which bank did you say you'd been to?'
'The TSB.'
'So that was a lie, in fact.'
'Yes.'
'Now, before we go any further, let me just impress upon you the serious nature of the problems facing you. If we ask you a question and you decide to lie about it, you're going to find yourself in some difficulty explaining why you lied.'
'Yes. I appreciate that.'

While Detective Sergeant Frank Anderson and his colleagues were interviewing Mr Spencer, Karen, the woman the taxi driver had seen being followed, was brought into the police station. It transpired that she was a friend of Angela's; they were near neighbours.

Karen was twenty and lived with her mother. Her house was about half a mile from the Rec. When she walked into the police station and began telling her story, it was obvious that she had been under considerable stress for a very long time. She sat with her head bowed and her hair hung over her face. She was in a state of deep shock, and looked numb. She was interviewed by a policewoman. She began, 'At about 2.30 a.m. today I walked up my road to Tollemache Road and I saw a man whom I have seen a number of times before, over the past three years. This man was sitting in a car facing down Tollemache Road towards the church. I walked up Tollemache Road towards the Rec and I saw this same man drive past me. I don't know where he went or where he parked his car, but he appeared again in front of me as I walked along. He walked in front of me all the way up to Tollemache Road, but he did not speak to me. Suddenly, as I got to near the BI School, he disappeared. I don't know where he went. Then, at about 5.30 a.m., I saw the same man again. He didn't speak and I walked past him, he followed me a little bit, but then disappeared. I don't know where he went.'

She decribed the man as about forty, well built with brown hair and she said he had a big brown car.

Detective Sergeant Frank Anderson finished his first interview with Mr Spencer around 1.30 p.m. He was pleased with how it had gone. As expected, Mr Spencer had admitted to none of the attacks, but he had revealed an awful lot about his background, details of which now needed to be checked.

Detective Sergeant Frank Anderson then went to speak to the policewoman who had been interviewing Karen and recalls, 'I was very surprised to discover that it appeared Spencer had been following Karen for about three years. It was quite obvious that she had suffered a great deal. We were surprised that she hadn't come forward before. We were very worried about her indeed. She needed help. It seemed Karen had more to tell us, but we had to proceed slowly and gently, she needed time.'

Unfortunately for the police time was something they were rapidly running out of because, as we saw in the last chapter, once a person has been arrested, officers have to follow strict procedures set down in the Police and Criminal Evidence Act 1986. This means they have only twenty-four hours in which to bring charges and, after this time has elapsed, the person must be released, unless there is an extremely good reason for keeping them at a police station. A further twelve hours can then be applied for, granted by the superintendent, after which only a magistrates' court, at a full hearing, can give permission for a person to be further detained.

Detective Sergeant Frank Anderson remembers, 'We had to move pretty quickly. We'd arrested Spencer at 6 a.m. so that was when the clock started. We'd pretty much exhausted our first line of questioning and were desperate for more information. We thought Karen might add something to her first statement during the course of the afternoon. Meanwhile, myself and another officer went to check out some of the details Spencer had told us. If we could disprove any of it then it would be something further to put to him. We visited his work and his home.'

Paul Spencer and his family lived in a semidetached house that they were buying from the council. When his wife was told about her husband's arrest, she could not understand what was happening. Detective Sergeant Frank Anderson went to visit her later in the day and remembers that 'She was very quiet when I spoke to her. I don't think she had really grasped the seriousness of the situation. She had all the children to look after and one of them was ill. We had to search the house and take some of Paul's things away for forensic examination. It must have been a great shock for her.'

Sergeant Frank Anderson also had to go through with her some of the details that had arisen from Mr Spencer's interview, checking them for accuracy – the times he said he had left for work, whether or not he was punctual and arrived home on time, particularly in the mornings. It seemed that everything was exactly as Mr Spencer had explained. However, his wife was very often asleep when he returned home in the early hours, so she was unable to confirm or deny whether he was ever late home. In fact, she could not remember what time he had gone to work that morning because she had been asleep.

When he got back to the police station, Detective Sergeant Frank Anderson held a briefing with the other officers. They went through what had happened and discovered that Karen had made another statement: 'I first recall this man about three years ago. He used to drive an old-fashioned car. It was tatty and a dirty white colour. I don't know the makes of cars. I saw this car about two or three times with the same man driving it. It would be between 2.30 a.m. and 3.30 a.m. It never stopped at first, but just used to drive slowly in front of me. I saw the car once at about 5 p.m. when it was parked. I was walking past an alleyway when the driver jumped out and grabbed me. He pulled me into the alley and said something in an angry voice. I cannot remember what words he used, but he frightened me. Once he got me in the alley, he did not touch me, he just let me go.'

Karen then moved house and it was nearly six months later before she saw him again: 'I would walk around in the night, usually in Birkenhead town centre, and around the precinct. I started to see the same man driving around. He was following me again. At this time he had a big brown car – again I don't know the make. He must have been following me around Birkenhead for a year and a half.'

She went on to explain, 'On some of the occasions when he followed me around he would stop and get out of his car. He would talk to me and try to be friends. I did talk to him, but I was always frightened of him. I did tell my mum about him. I remember a few months ago it was about 5.30 a.m. and I was walking through the park towards town when I was grabbed from behind. I started to scream and managed to glance behind me. It was the man who'd been following me. He forced me on to the grass.' He then indecently assaulted her.

Karen was obviously finding the interview deeply distressing and it was decided not to interview her any more that day. Detective Sergeant Frank Anderson recalls, 'We still felt Karen had more to tell us, but she needed a break. We took her home and arranged for her to come back the next day, Monday. We were concerned for her. She had a strange lifestyle, walking the streets at night. There was never any hint of prostitution but for some reason she spent hours walking around town in the middle of the night. She had previous convictions for carrying an offensive weapon. This she'd never used, but had it in her handbag to protect her. We never really got to the bottom of why she spent so many hours walking alone at night.'

It was now 6 p.m. and Detective Sergeant Frank Anderson and his colleague decided it was time to interview Mr Spencer once more. They had more information to put to him:

'Is there anything which you feel, now that you've had time to think about, that you wish to tell us which is possibly different from the last interview?'
'No.'
'Now, we have a statement from a female who states she saw you some time around 2.30 a.m. this morning in Tollemache Road.'
'Well, that's wrong, that's totally wrong. I categorically deny that I was out of the house at that time, in fact, I was asleep at that time.'
'Now, will it surprise you if I tell you that this female

*states she recognizes you as somebody she has seen for
the last three years who follows her, has been following
her around over a period of time and, in fact, may have
indecently assaulted her some three months ago in
Birkenhead Park?'*

'I haven't followed any girl.'

*'This young lady isn't one of those who says she was
raped some months ago. She's telling us she had some
contact with you. She's seen you on numerous occasions.
You've been following her. She will be in a position to
identify you if it comes to that. If you have knocked
around with her and there are no criminal offences
involved why not tell us about it ... if it comes out later
by other means, i.e. identification or anything else,
you've got problems explaining why.'*

'Yeah, but I haven't.'

'You haven't.'

*'I haven't been with that girl. She may have seen me, but
I have not been with that girl.'*

Detective Sergeant Frank Anderson then went over again
with Mr Spencer what he had done that morning – what
time he had arrived at work, who he had seen in
Birkenhead town centre, what his plans for the day
were. Mr Spencer's explanation remained consistent
throughout.

Detective Sergeant Frank Anderson then explained to
him that several items of clothing had been taken away
from his house for forensic examination. He also asked
him if he would be prepared to stand on an identification parade if necessary. Mr Spencer said he would.

Detective Sergeant Frank Anderson then put to Mr
Spencer details that had come from the taxi driver:

*'I have a statement here from a taxi driver which states
that he saw you watching or following a young lady and
he recognized that young lady as being the same one as
he saw last night. The thing is he found out this young*

lady's first name and he's seen her about numerous times, and that's why this morning when he saw her and saw you it clicked into place and he contacted the police. His impression was that you were following her.'

'You're wrong with that.'

'So, just for the records, you're denying following any young lady today?'

'Most definitely.'

'Have you ever been on Bidstone Hill with a young lady?'

'No. Not at all.'

'So, if anyone says that to the contrary then they're lying. Is that right?'

'Yes. I've not been on Bidstone Hill with anybody.'

'And you know nothing about these rapes whatsoever?'

'Nothing.'

The interview ended at 7 p.m. Shortly after this, Paul Spencer was released on police bail. Detective Sergeant Frank Anderson explains: 'The only way we could keep Spencer inside was to apply for an extension to keep him for a further twelve hours from the magistrates' court, but there was no point in doing this because we didn't have enough information at that time to warrant further detention. We had exhausted our line of questioning. However I was quite happy with how things had progressed. I was very confident that this was our man, and what we needed to do next was organize an identification parade. He looked so like the Photofit that I felt confident the victims would pick him out.'

The identification parade was what the police were hanging all their hopes on. Mr Spencer had not admitted to any of the allegations, neither was there any forensic evidence, and it was unlikely that the clothes taken from Mr Spencer's home would reveal anything either. However if one, or maybe two, victims could identify Mr Spencer as their attacker, then this would add enormous weight to the prosecution's case. Without it, the investigation would almost certainly collapse.

The next morning, Monday, a briefing was held in Detective Chief Inspector Chris Kemp's office. He was delighted with the events of the weekend and Detective Sergeant Frank Anderson filled him in on all the details. He explained that Mr Spencer had made no admissions, but there were a number of striking coincidences. The taxi driver and Karen had both described the two cars – a white Maxi and a brown Volvo. Spencer looked remarkably like the Photofit, and his explanation of what he had been doing on Sunday morning was bizarre to say the least. He went on, 'I can't understand why Spencer deliberately drove the long way round from work. Why didn't he just go into work a little earlier than usual? Instead, he stopped in Birkenhead to buy a newspaper, he then lied about needing to go to the bank. After this he drove a little further and parked up to read his newspaper. He then had to drive all the way home just to get another shirt, and he had to be back at work for 8.30 a.m. In my mind he's definitely covering something up.'

Detective Chief Inspector Chris Kemp agreed that Mr Spencer's actions certainly seemed strange and did not appear to make sense. From the details the victims had given, and the background information from Mr Spencer himself, it seemed that he had every opportunity to carry out these attacks. He worked irregular hours, sometimes into the early hours of the morning, and his wife never knew exactly what time he got in. His description fitted precisely. So, it was decided to organize the identification parade as quickly as possible.

Meanwhile, that same Monday morning, Karen had been brought back to the police station and she was making another statement. She said that six weeks after the first attack, she met the man again in Birkenhead Park by the lake: 'He dragged me on to the grass by the rocks. I was screaming and he put his hand over my mouth. I bit his finger. He then forced me on to the floor and tied my hands behind my back with what looked like a maroon tie.' Moments later, she was raped.

Detective Sergeant Frank Anderson recalls, 'We knew Karen had been keeping something back and now finally she had admitted the full truth of what had happened. It was deeply distressing for her and, although her case greatly strengthened the inquiry, before proceeding any further we decided to seek an expert's opinion on how she would cope giving evidence in court.'

Despite this new rape allegation, it was decided not to bring Mr Spencer back in for questioning until after the identification parade. He would only deny the charge, and it would be stronger if they could put this, together with the results of the identification parade, to him at one interview.

Detective Chief Inspector Chris Kemp remembers, 'It was a very difficult time for us. Instinctively we felt we had the right man, but we had not a shred of evidence against him. We could never take the case to court on what little information we had. It seemed everything was going to hinge on the identification parade, and even then we ideally needed forensic evidence to be sure of a conviction.'

Ten days later, 6 August 1991, the identification parade was held at Wallasey police station. The only victim who could not attend was Karen because she was out of the area.

Nine men stood in a line behind a one-way mirror; Mr Spencer was at position number five. All the investigating officers waited in another part of the building because, by law, they are not allowed to be in the same room as the witnesses; if at any time they are, then the parade is declared null and void.

Detective Sergeant Frank Anderson remembers, 'It was a very tense time for us. We had played our final card and were desperate to know the results immediately. I had spent weeks on this case and today was going to be make or break. I kept everything crossed.'

All the victims were very nervous as they waited outside. Jane, who had been attacked nearly nine months earlier, burst into tears as she walked along the line. She ran out of the room saying she could not go through it all again. She could not face giving evidence in court. She did not pick him out.

Angela, the schoolgirl, was next. This time, without any hesitation, she said that the man who had raped her was standing at number five. Claire went next and she, too, picked out Mr Spencer. The taxi driver also positively identified him.

When they heard the results, the investigation team were ecstatic and, immediately afterwards, Paul Spencer was formally arrested for two offences of rape.

Detective Sergeant Frank Anderson recalls, 'We were delighted. It was the best result we could have hoped for. Chris Kemp and I discussed how we should approach the interview. We could be stronger in our line of questioning now that the victims had picked him out. We had to try and break down his story. We decided Chris should ask the majority of questions this time because I'd conducted all the earlier interviews.'

Detective Chief Inspector Chris Kemp began:

'The date is the 6th of August, and the time is 8.15 p.m. I'm going to caution you. You do not have to say anything unless you wish to do so, but what you say may be given in evidence. I have been investigating since early April a series of sexual attacks on young women in the north end of Birkenhead. Those enquiries have led us to bring you to the police station today to be put on an identification parade, which you went on willingly. I was not present at the identification parade as part of the investigation team, but I have seen statements from two

girls who went to the parade. They identified you positively as the person who was responsible for raping them. Do you want to make any comment?'

'I explained to my solicitor in the cell prior to coming into the interview room that I want to cooperate fully with the investigations and come clean and be honest relating to the whole affair. I was responsible for attacking that girl on the Rec. However, I dispute penetration.'

Detective Sergeant Frank Anderson was amazed that he had admitted his guilt so quickly and remembered that, 'His whole persona had changed and he was a completely different person to the man I'd first interviewed. He was very nervous, and he looked like his world had collapsed. He sat staring at the floor as he spoke.'

Mr Spencer then went on to describe how he had sexually assaulted Claire. After this admission, Detective Chief Inspector Chris Kemp questioned him about Angela, the schoolgirl, who said she was raped on Bidstone Hill. Mr Spencer said: 'I walked behind her and pulled her into Bidstone Hill, there was a little struggle when she screamed and begged me not to hurt her. I said I wasn't going to hurt her but I wanted her to come with me. I took her up through the bushes into Bidstone Hill and when we got to a fairly secluded spot, I asked her to remove the bottom half of her clothing.' It was here that he raped her.

Detective Chief Inspector Chris Kemp then went on to talk about the other incidents that they had been investigating. He asked Mr Spencer if he was going to talk about those as well:

'No. I state categorically now and I stated to my solicitor earlier that the only two people that I've been involved with are those two people that we've just talked about and they were both one after the other.'

'Well, let's go on to Karen. Unfortunately she was unable to be here this afternoon, but the taxi driver was

*and he identified you as being the person he had seen
following her on numerous occasions.'*

'No.'

*'Karen made a statement in relation to that person, who
we believe to be you, and in that statement there is an
allegation of rape in Birkenhead Park.'*

*'No. The only two girls that I've attacked are those girls
that you've mentioned earlier. I have not attacked any
other girl at all.'*

Mr Spencer said that he had seen the girls walking along
when he was driving home from work, and just decided
there and then he was going to attack them. He had not
followed them for any distance. He had acted on the
spur of the moment. He continually denied attacking
anyone else. At the end of the interview, he stressed that
the reason he had admitted the two offences was because
he did not want to cause the girls further misery by making them relive their ordeal in court.

Detective Chief Inspector Chris Kemp remembers, 'To
use a common parlance in this part of the world, Spencer
was absolutely "gobsmacked" when he was picked out
at the identification parade. When we went in to do the
interview, he looked like the bottom had fallen out of his
world. He was a desperate man. The game was up and
his best way of getting out of it was to hold his hands up
to the two that had identified him and to deny the ones
that hadn't. He expressed a great deal of regret for what
he'd done and said he just had the urge to do it.'

Mr Spencer only ever admitted these two crimes, and
when another identification parade was held weeks later
and Karen picked him out, he repeatedly denied the
charges.

Detective Sergeant Frank Anderson remembers, 'He
had recovered himself so much better this time round.
He was articulate and not fazed by anything I said. He
stood by his original statement.'

In court, thirty-seven-year-old Paul Spencer pleaded guilty to two charges: one for the rape of the schoolgirl, Angela, and the other for indecently assaulting Claire. On 11 May 1992, he was sentenced to a total of seven and a half years' imprisonment. He had no previous convictions.

Detective Chief Inspector Chris Kemp said, 'We were prepared to take Karen's case through the courts because we felt it was so strong. However, when we received the psychiatrist's report in relation to her on the viability of giving evidence, we were advised against putting her through the ordeal of court because of the trauma she had suffered. Although seven and a half years might sound a lot, I think if we had got a successful prosecution of her case, the sentence would have been significantly higher. However, the result of this inquiry was still much better than I could ever have hoped for. With all the problems we had, I think it was quite an achievement'.

Afterwards, from his prison cell, Paul Spencer wrote letters to the victims, apologizing for what he had done. He gave no reasons for his actions.

4

DOUBLE
'SUPERGRASS'

A fourteen-year-old boy turned on his video to watch *Top of the Pops* but saw that *Crimewatch* had been recorded instead. It was two days after the programme had been broadcast, Saturday 16 November 1985, and he found himself watching a reconstruction of a robbery where gunmen were strapping a remote-control device to the back of a security guard. He stopped the tape and replayed it; there was no doubt in his mind that he had seen this device some months earlier. He called his mother and together they phoned the police.

This boy was to give the first clue in what was to become a two-and-a-half-year police investigation that made criminal history.

Broxbourne, in Hertfordshire, is an attractive, semi-rural commuter town just north of the M25 and about thirty miles from central London. One summer's afternoon in 1985, the fourteen-year-old boy and his friends were playing near their home in Broxbourne when they saw a pile of rubbish sacks lying on the pavement by the front wall of a house. They looked inside and found a face mask, false hair, glue, a small radio receiver, two hundred cigarettes and a home-made electronic device.

The boy collected junk and he took part of the contents of the bags home. He wore the face mask for a laugh, but this frightened his mother and she made him throw it away. He kept the electronic device and fiddled

133

with it for some weeks. When he stripped it down, he realized that it was a remote-control device, similar to one he had installed in a toy racing car, but, not realizing its significance, he eventually threw it away.

During this part of 1985, police officers from the Flying Squad in London were very busy. Detective Constable Kevin Shapland joined the Squad on 1 September.

It is a great honour to be accepted into this élite group, which investigates major armed robbery offences in London. There are only four offices in the whole of the capital with a total of 140 officers, chosen from a possible four thousand officers in the whole of the Metropolitan area. Advertisements are placed annually and only around twenty officers are selected.

The Flying Squad was set up at the end of the First World War when there was great concern in London regarding the dramatic increase in serious crime. During the war, a large number of ordinary men had been taught to kill, maim and accept violence as a normal part of life. They returned from overseas restless and unable to settle again to a normal style of living. In October 1918, twelve detectives were summoned to the New Scotland Yard office of Detective Chief Inspector Frederick Wensley and told that they were to form an experimental group to combat the serious increase in crime, and, for the first time, they were given authority to operate anywhere in London.

At the end of the first year, their results were so impressive that they were retained as a permanent section. Two years later, a journalist, W. G. T. Crook, referred to this group as a 'flying squad of picked detectives' and so he has been credited as the man who christened the Flying Squad.

As their success over the years increased, so did their numbers. The Flying Squad had not initially been intended to investigate particular crimes as such; its main purpose was to concentrate on serious organized crime of all natures. However, since 1978, the squad has been tasked to investigate major armed robbery offences in London and arrest professional criminals committing such crimes.

In 1985, there seemed to be a wealth of armed robberies, ranging from banks and building societies to cash in transit (security vans) and post offices. Detective Constable Kevin Shapland's first major inquiry occurred shortly after he joined the squad and concerned a robbery in Tottenham, north London. This stood out from other cases being investigated because it was unusual and more serious – guns were fired, hostages taken and a bomb used. It happened on Friday 13 September.

Imperial Cold Stores was a hops warehouse in Tottenham. It was a windowless red brick building, situated at the end of a cul-de-sac, and there were only a few deliveries each week because it was due to close at the end of the year. There was a skeleton staff of about twenty, and Fred was the gateman. He arrived, as usual, at 7 a.m. Peter, a lorry driver, was sleeping in his cab in the yard. He had driven through the night to avoid the traffic and was resting before picking up his load.

Fred switched off the alarm and went to fill up the kettle when, suddenly, he heard a noise and, within seconds, there was a gun pointing at him. Two men had burst in, threatened him and made him sit at his desk by the window to wait for the security van, which was due any minute. Fred had a heart condition and said he was not well, but this made little difference.

At 8 a.m. the van arrived. It was the first delivery of the day and the driver nodded at Fred who was sitting in the window. Fred smiled back – he could do little else with a sawn-off shotgun pointing straight at him. The robbers demanded Fred's car keys and told him to act normally as two of the guards came towards the office door. As soon as they came inside, they were overpowered and one of the guards was forced to have a remote-control device strapped to his back. He was told to take a cup of tea to his colleague outside in the van. The robbers went with him.

During the attack, an employee saw the robbery and tried to struggle with one of the gunmen, who fired a shot. The employee was lucky to escape unharmed. A few minutes later, the company's director arrived. He was dragged from his car and a warning shot was fired by his side. The gunmen used his car for their getaway. They unstrapped the device from the guard and made off with £90 000.

The police noticed a number of similarities between this robbery and three other attempted robberies that had taken place in Hertfordshire during the last six months. On 24 April, at Enfield Crematorium, three armed suspects had taken staff hostage as they lay in wait for a security van to arrive. The time of delivery had changed, and the suspects left empty-handed. On 3 May, at the Cross & Herbert site in Hoddesdon, two armed suspects held staff hostage as they lay in wait for a security van. On its arrival, the van's crew was so unhappy because everywhere was too quiet that they left without making a delivery, so the suspects fled empty-handed. On 27 June at Amtico, Enfield, three armed suspects went into a warehouse, held staff hostage and waited for a security van to arrive. The van failed to turn up and, once again, the gang left empty-handed.

Although these were only attempts there were a number of remarkable coincidences:

- they had all happened early in the morning
- the premises seemed irrelevant because the target was always the security van
- the weapons and descriptions of the offenders were all the same.

It was becoming apparent that a single, sophisticated team of armed robbers was responsible for these offences, and it was quite clear that they would go to any lengths to achieve their objectives.

Following the armed robbery in Tottenham, which received a great deal of media interest, a *Crimewatch* researcher telephoned Detective Constable Kevin Shapland with a view to filming a reconstruction.

Although the programme was only in its second year of transmission, the cases featured then were chosen in much the same way as they are today.

Sometimes police officers ring the BBC production team direct, but mostly the programme's four researchers scour all the newspapers – including the thirty regional papers that are delivered each day – to find the right kinds of cases for the programme. It is essential that they each have strong points of appeal or clues such as details of cars seen in the area, a possible artist's impression of the villains, together with descriptions of their weapons.

When appealing to an audience of eleven million people each month, it is essential to have something the viewer can latch on to, whether it be a face they might recognize, a number plate they might remember or whatever. It is factors like these that have made the programme so successful in solving one in five of its cases, and perhaps, too, this is why *Crimewatch* sometimes finds it difficult to get the right kinds of stories needed for the programme each month.

Once the researcher has spoken to the programme's producer about the case – usually at the monthly production meeting – a director goes and meets the police, witnesses, and, in some cases, the victims. The director spends several days looking closely at all the details, and then another meeting is arranged with the producer to discuss the final structure of the film.

Not only are the filmed reconstructions expensive,

they require an enormous amount of time and meticulous planning, by both the *Crimewatch* team and the police. Precise locations are nearly always used and sometimes this can create enormous difficulties, especially if the time is at night and the place is a busy road junction. Every detail, though, however minor, must be accurate because this might jog the viewer's memory and so solve the crime. A police liaison officer is always on location when the filming takes place, to check everything as it is filmed.

Once a researcher had contacted Detective Constable Kevin Shapland regarding the robbery in Tottenham, north London, a meeting was arranged, and it was decided to film a reconstruction.

The item was broadcast on 14 November 1985. There were far fewer people watching that evening than would normally be expected because the Miss World contest was being shown on ITV, so only 60 calls came in to the studio, compared with an average of about 150 for a filmed reconstruction. Officers back at the incident room did not have much luck either; the response was pretty poor. None of the calls provided immediate excitement – most gave possible names for the suspects and details of where the bomb had come from. The device left at the scene of the Cross & Herbert robbery was shown in the studio, and this was similar to the one used at Tottenham.

Then, two days after the programme, the schoolboy from Broxbourne contacted his local police station. At first, nothing much was thought of the call and, as a matter of routine, a detective telephoned the Flying Squad and spoke to Detective Constable Kevin Shapland. He asked him to visit the boy, and suggested that he get him to draw the device he had seen some months earlier. Then, if it looked nothing like the bomb they were investigating, his information could be quickly eliminated.

When the officer arrived at the boy's house, he duly asked him to draw what he had found and, without any prompting, he correctly drew the four wooden corner blocks that were inside the bomb. This was remarkable because the inside of the bomb had never been shown before; these details had not been released by the police.

It was the first major breakthrough in the investigation. Detective Constable Kevin Shapland remembers, 'It was incredible that this boy, whilst flicking through a video tape, had latched on to the very point where the bomb was displayed on *Crimewatch*. He was able to give us an address where the device had been found, and there is no doubt that without this information we would never have looked at that house in a million years.'

The house was called 'Emerald' and was, in fact, the name given to a bungalow in a very desirable area of Broxbourne. The police soon discovered that the present owners, David and Rita Croke, had only just moved in and had no previous convictions for major crimes. However, the previous owners had moved into a considerably bigger house in Broxbourne and owned an electrical and building company in Highbury. It was this information that made police focus their attention on them. Detective Constable Kevin Shapland recalls, 'I was working a little bit as a one-man band at this time, pecking away at it whenever I could. There were simply not enough hours in the day to do everything. Sometimes I would sit outside the business premises in Highbury and other days I would drive past "Emerald". I couldn't sit outside the house because it was in a cul-de-sac with a dead end, so I just used to note down vehicle numbers and try as much as possible to have a look at the people coming and going.'

Nearly four weeks after the *Crimewatch* reconstruction, on 11 December 1985, a robbery at Armaguard Security Depot in Essex added a new dimension to the investigation.

Joe was a key-holder and security guard for Armaguard. On 10 December, he finished work and arrived home in his white Lada at about 7 p.m. He opened the door and went into the living room where he was confronted by two men with shotguns and balaclavas. His wife and daughter were handcuffed to the dining room table. The robbers said that if he complied with everything, nobody would get hurt. They continued, 'You know what we're here for. We want to take you up to the depot tomorrow and you can open the safe.'

One of the robbers told Joe that he had a remote-control bomb and showed him a box with a red light on top. He said that this would be strapped to a member of his family and, if he did not carry out all their instructions, it would be detonated. Even though Joe was terrified, he showed remarkable courage. He had been a prisoner of war of the Japanese and this perhaps helped him to keep his nerve. He realized that there was no way out now and so he decided to be as cooperative as possible with the two robbers, who sat beside him throughout the night. A third member of the gang was outside with a radio. He kept in constant touch with his colleagues, using different code names, and it sounded to Joe like his whole house was surrounded. As preparations were made to leave the house, Joe pleaded with the robbers to strap the bomb to him instead. This they agreed to do and, when they left the house at 5.30 p.m. the bomb was fitted underneath Joe's car seat.

Joe's wife and thirty-year-old daughter were left tied up inside the house so that they could not raise the alarm. Joe drove his car to the security depot and the robbers followed. They waited in the yard for about an hour until two other guards arrived, one of whom had the keys to the premises. Joe got out and joined the others by the front door of the building. As they were about to go in, the robbers came up from behind, threatened them and told them to keep quiet, then forced them to open the door. Once inside, they tied up the guards and made them lie on the floor while Joe was forced to open the strongroom. After the cash bags had been loaded, Joe and his colleagues were put into the strongroom and the door was locked. The gunmen escaped with half a million pounds in a white Honda van.

The robbers left the bomb still attached to Joe's car and later, when the police examined it, it turned out to be a dummy.

For Essex police, this was the biggest robbery ever committed on their patch. Detective Constable Kevin Shapland was seconded to work with them for a week to look for similarities that might link it to his other cases: 'To be honest, I wasn't convinced that this one was connected. It seemed to have been better planned. It must have taken ages to get all the family research on Joe, and this time the hostages had been held overnight. Added to this, they used a dummy device which was left on the car – why would they suddenly switch from a viable electrical device to a dummy?'

Two months later, Detective Constable Kevin Shapland was driving past 'Emerald' on his way home from work when he saw three cars in the driveway: an Audi GT, a Porsche and a Nissan Sunny Estate. Checks on the latter revealed that it belonged to Dolly Ince, wife of George Ince.

Dolly Ince had previously been married to Charles Kray, brother of the Kray twins. She married George Ince in 1977. He was escorted to the ceremony from Wormwood Scrubs prison where he was serving a sentence for armed robbery. He was well known to the police and had completed his time a few years ago.

This information was vital to the investigation. Why would George or Dolly Ince be at 'Emerald' with the Crokes? The fact that they had been spotted together changed the whole direction of the inquiry. The police's first hunch regarding the previous owners of 'Emerald' was completely wrong, and attention now concentrated on the present occupants, David and Rita Croke.

A surveillance team began watching the house and, in particular, David Croke. 'Operation Standard' was launched.

David Croke was forty-three and had minor convictions for shoplifting some seven years ago. His wife, Rita, was twelve years older than him and they had been married for about fifteen years. Rita had children from her first marriage.

David had left school at fourteen without any qualifications and had held various casual jobs driving vehicles, but he was unemployed at that time.

From the middle of April 1977 until February 1985, he had lived in a council flat in Edmonton, London N9. It was in February that he moved to 'Emerald' and he paid the purchase price in cash – £85 000. The transaction was in the name of his wife, Rita Croke.

The police were immediately suspicious of this deal. Croke had no visible means of income, yet he had recently bought an expensive house. Detectives spent several months observing his movements, but he kept himself to himself and rarely ventured out. It was not until the summer that their patience was finally rewarded.

At the end of July, a green Golf GTI was seen in the driveway of 'Emerald', and the man driving it was white and six feet tall. Detectives were discussing who this might be in the office the next day, when one officer, who had been observing a well-known 'supergrass' – Donald Barrett – remembered that he drove a similar car. Mr Barrett had many previous convictions for armed robbery and had been released from prison three years earlier. In 1980, he was given a reduced prison sentence when he cooperated with the police and gave evidence against his co-accused in a case of armed robbery.

Pictures of Mr Barrett were shown to fellow officers and it was quickly confirmed that the man police had seen outside 'Emerald' was indeed Donald Barrett. This was a major breakthrough because police had now identified two well-known armed robbers in the company of David Croke.

Detective Superintendent Duncan MacRae was put in charge of the investigation: 'We began to move into a more proactive role because here was one of the foremost armed robbers in the London area. He was obviously an associate of David Croke's and quite capable of committing all the robberies we were linking, including the Armaguard job.'

At this time, the police had no idea what the team were planning, but, a week later, the first real signs of activity began. Mr Barrett arrived at 'Emerald' one afternoon in his green Golf GTI. He went inside for a short time and then came out with David Croke. They both got into the Golf and Mr Barrett drove the car away. The surveillance team followed behind. They headed towards London, went straight through the city centre and on to Battersea. They passed Battersea Dogs' Home on the right, then turned left off the main road into an industrial estate. The police waited outside. They watched the car drive slowly round the block and come out again.

Situated in the far corner was a security depot called Shields. It specialized in the transportation of monies and valuables, and police immediately became suspicious that this could be the gang's next target. Observations and intelligence over the next few days seemed to confirm that it was.

In these circumstances, it would be normal for the police to liaise with the security depot staff and explain to them what was happening. The police would then have access to rooms for observation purposes, and an enormous amount of planning could be coordinated from within the premises. However, in this case, events began to unfold in such a way that it was impossible for the police to alert Shields without risking the whole operation.

A detective was walking past the depot one morning when he noticed a black Golf parked outside the front entrance, which immediately caught his attention. He had seen this car a few days earlier in the driveway at 'Emerald', and the owner had been traced to an Alan Turner who lived in Essex. The detective's first thought was that the robbers had an inside agent. Mr Turner was observed over the next few days and the detective's initial thoughts were confirmed – he was indeed working for Shields, but they had no idea in what capacity.

This created a major problem for the police. Not only did they not know what his duties were, but, at this stage, it was impossible to know whether or not anyone else from the company was involved with the armed team. It was because of this that they dare not contact anyone from within the Shields company itself.

Detective Superintendent Duncan MacRae held an urgent meeting. It was obvious that the staff from Shields would be placed in some danger if the inquiry continued. The pros and cons of the whole investigation were discussed – should they call it off just when the gang were coming within their grasp?

It was decided that if they did abort, then the robbery team would inevitably go and attack somewhere else and, possibly, then the target would be unknown to them. More people would be put at risk. At least here they had some control over the situation.

After several meetings between senior officers, it was decided to continue with the plans. Arresting one of the most dangerous armed gangs in London had to be the priority, and with so much information already, it was too good an opportunity to miss.

The police knew that they were looking at a potential

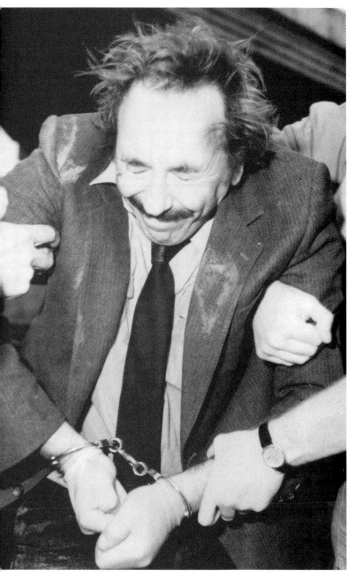

David Croke at the moment of arrest. (*Double Supergrass*)

RIGHT: Kidnap victim Stephanie Slater arriving at Nottingham Crown Court to give evidence in the trial of Michael Sams. (*Murderer's Game*)

BELOW: The interior of Michael Sams' workshop where Stephanie Slater was held hostage. (*Murderer's Game*)

The artist's impression of Michael Sams as shown on *Crimewatch UK*. (*Murderer's Game*)

Michael Sams. (*Murderer's Game*)

Ronald Harrison (above, left) victim of a vicious murder. (*A Chapter of Revelations*).

John Calton alias Karl Schultz (above, right) has never returned to his true identity and has retained his German accent following his imprisonment for robbery and kidnapping. *Double Identity*)

OPPOSITE PAGE
Using evidence like the scrap of newspaper (above) police were able to establish a connection between David Wynne Roberts (below, right) and the death of Bronwen Nixon (below, left).
The Red Connection)

ABOVE: 'Emerald', where David and Rita Croke lived. (*Double 'Supergrass'*)

RIGHT: The kitchen where Fred was attacked. (*Double 'Supergrass'*)

Gold bullion recovered from the M1 raid. (*Double 'Supergrass'*)

'The Rec', Birkenhead. (*Birkenhead Serial Rapist*)

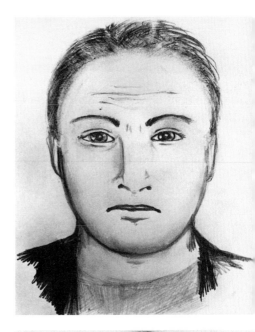

The striking similarity between the Photofit (below) and the drawing (above) by one of the victims, helped establish the identity of the Birkenhead rapist. (*Birkenhead Serial Rapist*)

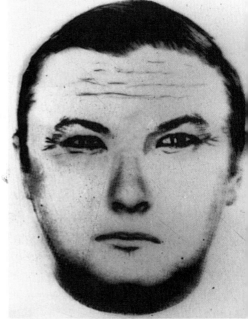

hostage situation, so every move the robbers might make had to be meticulously planned for.

The first task for the police was to find a number of observation points around the industrial estate from which they could watch the main entrance of Shields unnoticed. This proved quite difficult because the depot backed on to a railway line at one end, and the main vantage point was a pub, several hundred yards away. However, the only way on to the industrial estate was from the busy Battersea Road and, luckily, on the junction was an old disused police station that provided the ideal spot to see everything that came and went. A school in the far corner of the estate, overlooking the main yard, was another observation point and, because it was the school holidays, the caretaker was the only person around: 'It was very difficult not to draw attention to ourselves at this time. It was a small estate and if anyone from any of the other offices had been aware of our presence, then word would have got around. I needed to find places that were far enough away, yet, at the same time, had a clear view of the whole area.' It took Detective Constable Kevin Shapland several days to find all the locations.

Information that was coming in from the intelligence teams suggested that the raid was going to happen any day now. Donald Barrett and David Croke were frequently seen together, and police assumed that they were finalizing their plans. Everyone was prepared for an imminent move when, suddenly, Mr Barrett flew out of the country to Portugal with his family. This left officers in limbo until two days later – Sunday 10 August – when Barrett was seen to arrive back at Heathrow by himself. The surveillance team followed him to 'Emerald' in Broxbourne where he met up with David Croke. The two men then drove immediately to Alan Turner's house in Essex and the police could only assume that this must be the final planning meeting. They were together for only a few hours, and by 10 p.m. Mr Croke and Mr Barrett had returned to 'Emerald'.

Detective Constable Kevin Shapland briefed officers that evening at Lambeth police station. He showed them plans for the depot, and the full details of the operation were discussed.

That night, the weather was atrocious; violent thunderstorms hit Hertfordshire and this made it difficult for the surveillance team watching movements at the house. The armed operation was planned throughout the night. Officers from the PT17 Blue Berets – the tactical firearms unit – were stationed around the depot in Battersea, as their skills in both hostage situations and firearms were essential. Officers attached to the Flying Squad, skilled in mobile surveillance, were on standby just in case they had to follow and arrest elsewhere. A total of eighty officers were on duty that night and radio silence was maintained.

Detective Superintendent Duncan MacRae was away and, in his absence, Detective Chief Superintendent Peter Gwynn assumed charge of the operation. He recalled: 'We knew there was likely to be a hostage situation similar to the Armaguard robbery and my job was a containment one: let the suspects in and then seal off the whole area.'

The first indication that something might be happening was at 4.20 a.m. when the outside lights of 'Emerald' were suddenly turned on. Donald Barrett and David Croke walked out, got into their car and drove down the road to a lock-up garage. They emerged a few minutes later in a different vehicle – a blue Ford Escort van. Both men were wearing dark suits, ties and carrying a holdall and radio. They drove towards Battersea, south London.

Detective Constable Kevin Shapland remembers, 'I was in the police station observation point, overlooking the main Battersea road, and when we heard they were *en route*, my stomach turned. The adrenalin began to pump, and I just hoped that after all this preparation everything would go according to plan.'

At 5.45 a.m. Alan Turner arrived for work at the depot in his Golf and, several minutes later, he was seen chatting to his colleagues who had parked next to him. At this stage, the police still had no idea what position Mr Turner held in the company or, indeed, what was going to happen next. They did not know whether his colleague was innocent or not, as it was possible that he, too, was one of the gang. Mr Turner looked nervous – he was pacing up and down, smoking heavily.

About ten minutes later, the blue Ford Escort van with Mr Barrett and Mr Croke inside drove on to the industrial estate. Immediately in front of them, was the key-holder of Shields, driving a Vauxhall car, totally unaware that he was being followed. They were heading towards the security depot.

The Vauxhall stopped outside the gates, and the driver got out and greeted Mr Turner and his colleague. The blue van drove slowly towards them and the police thought that this was going to be the moment of attack. Everyone stood by, waiting, but, instead of stopping, the blue van kept going. It drove back out of the estate into a street nearby where it parked.

The atmosphere was very tense at the police observation points. What were the two robbers doing? Why had they driven off the estate? Detective Constable Kevin Shapland recalls, 'You could feel the mood change. Trying to judge what they would do next, and be prepared for it was almost impossible. I was really tense and very worried. Nobody in the office spoke – we just watched and waited.'

Meanwhile, back at Shields, Mr Turner and his colleague had gone inside with the key-holder. They emerged a few minutes later and Mr Turner walked towards a white security van parked by the main gates. He was carrying something that resembled a shoe box, and he opened the back doors and put it inside. He then jumped into the van, his colleague got into the passenger seat and they started up the engine.

Suddenly, the police realized that Mr Turner's job was, in fact, that of a security guard and, as he reversed out of the yard and drove away from the depot, the police's worst fear came true. The target was not going to be Shields after all, but they had no idea what it actually was, what was going to happen next or what was in the back of the security van.

Detective Chief Superintendent Peter Gwynn recalls, 'We now had a real problem because we had a vehicle with perhaps a considerable amount of commodity on board – money, cash, gold – and two armed robbers in the vicinity. We didn't know if the job had been called off or what. The only thing I could do was employ what vehicles I had in the area to follow the target vehicle.'

This, of course, amounted to a very small number because, as the depot was assumed to be the target, ninety-nine per cent of Detective Chief Superintendent Gwynn's team were surrounding that building and it was impossible for them to move from their present positions without alerting the whole neighbourhood. Detective Constable Kevin Shapland was part of the authorized firearms team and, as his observation point overlooked the main road, it was easy for him and a colleague to jump into a car and provide back-up to the surveillance crew. They followed some distance behind. Detective Constable Kevin Shapland remembers, 'All the plans we made had gone. We didn't know where we were going, we didn't know what Turner was carrying in the shoe box, and we had no idea where this was going to end. The blue Ford van with Barrett and Croke followed the security van and we were some distance behind. Barrett was wearing a wig and glasses. It was a bit frightening because we knew they were likely to be armed, and the situation could potentially be very dangerous.'

The convoy went round Hyde Park Corner and up the Edgware Road on to the M1 motorway. As a matter of urgency, command of the police operation was switched to the officer leading the surveillance team.

When police officers go outside their area with guns, then strict procedures have to be followed. Under normal circumstances, only the Assistant Chief Constable, and those above him, can give the authority for other officers to enter their county force carrying weapons. Then, very often, if a firearms team is needed, this would consist of officers from that particular force, even if the investigation team were based elsewhere.

Unfortunately, in this particular case, because events had changed so quickly and the police had no idea where they were going, county forces had to be alerted to the situation as the team were driving through their counties. Luckily, the Metropolitan police helicopter had been put on standby and was waiting at the Battersea heliport. Once the robbers drove out of the area, the helicopter was called to assist and it followed, about two miles behind the convoy.

The helicopter is equipped with radio equipment that enables it to link up immediately with any other force. It could also monitor the radio transmissions from the surveillance team. This was to prove invaluable because it relayed to each county headquarters and New Scotland Yard what was happening almost instantaneously.

The convoy had been travelling less than an hour when the white security van suddenly pulled off the motorway into the service station at Newport Pagnell. It was closely followed by the blue Escort van. It was now 7.45 a.m. Mr Turner parked the security van, got out and made his way towards the restaurant area. The surveillance cars parked outside the service area on the hard shoulder so as not to alert the suspects. They could see Mr Croke and Mr Barrett talking to Mr Turner outside the main entrance. It looked like this meeting had been prearranged.

Mr Turner then went inside and appeared again carrying two plastic coffee cups. As he walked back towards the security van, he was followed by Mr Croke and Mr Barrett. It seemed something was about to happen, but, because of where the van had parked, the police had poor visibility of the scene, and if they moved any closer, it might alert the robbers.

This particular location made it difficult for the surveillance team because if they mounted an attack in such an open place, it would have been very hard to contain. The fact that these suspects had previously taken hostages, fired guns and used bomb devices was of grave concern. In the car park were members of the public with their vehicles – a situation tailor made for hostage taking. So, it was decided not to attempt to make any arrests until such time that the robbery had taken place, unless danger to life dictated otherwise.

The white security van was next seen leaving the car park, heading towards the motorway, only this time, David Croke, not Alan Turner, was at the wheel and Mr Barrett was on his own, following closely behind in the blue van. It seemed that the robbers had taken charge. There was no sign of either guard. Something had obviously happened and police now had to act.

Officers knew that their best point of attack was the slip road leading back on to the motorway, but the timing was crucial. Any confrontation on the main carriageway could be fatal, so, as the two vans made their way towards the motorway, the attack signal was given.

The surveillance vehicles, parked on the hard shoulder, raced up the motorway in a hair-raising chase and arrived just as the white van was attempting to rejoin the M1. They forced it on to the nearside grass verge and, in seconds, officers with drawn firearms had pulled David Croke out of the van before he knew what was happening. When he tried to move his hand towards his jacket pocket, officers quickly grabbed and handcuffed him.

They searched him and found, among other things, a loaded .32 revolver, flick knife and CS gas canisters. He was wearing surgical gloves and a radio transmitter.

Mr Barrett attempted to drive away in the blue van and Detective Constable Kevin Shapland was one of the officers in the car that pursued him. When he saw he was surrounded, Mr Barrett stopped, got out of the van and put his hands in the air saying, 'Enough is enough.'

Donald Barrett was a professional criminal and, as soon as he realized that he was outnumbered, he gave himself up, even though he was carrying a firearm. He recognized one of the officers who arrested him and congratulated him, saying, 'Hello Phil, nice little tickle you've had here.'

Detective Constable Kevin Shapland remembers, 'When you get the word, it's like a release. We moved very fast and, once we'd got them on the ground, taken their weapons away and handcuffed them, it was a feeling of relief more than anything else that we're not hurt and nobody else is either – they're nicked.'

The two security guards were found hooded, lying face down on the floor of the security van. Mr Turner's wrists were lightly bound with plastic ties while his colleague wore handcuffs. Although it was obvious that Mr Turner was acting in concert with Mr Barrett and Mr Croke, the police still had no idea at this stage how innocent the second guard was. Inside the shoe box was gold bullion worth £283 000.

The four men were immediately taken to Milton Keynes police station, where they were detained. Initially, they were held incommunicado because police needed to go to a number of addresses and collect possible evidence before anyone was alerted to the arrests.

At 2 p.m. officers arrived at 'Emerald', just as Rita Croke was getting into her car. Officers arrested her and searched the car. Inside were two bags and, when asked what was in them, she said, 'Rubbish, I'm dumping it.'

One bag contained a Reck .65 handgun, one bullet, gas pellets, shotgun cartridges, spectacles, correspondence and adhesive. The other bag contained a holster, a bullet, hats and clothing.

She, too, was taken to Milton Keynes police station and initially charged with conspiracy to rob.

It soon transpired that Alan Turner had worked for Shields since 1 July 1986 and was the son of Rita Croke. He was charged with robbery and firearms offences. The other guard was entirely innocent.

Attention now centred on Donald Barrett. The Flying Squad suspected that the gang had been involved in other similarly planned robberies, but, without Mr Barrett's help, it was going to be difficult to prove this. So, Detective Constable Kevin Shapland and another officer went into Mr Barrett's cell and began to sow the seeds of him being a 'supergrass' for the second time, something that had never before happened in criminal history.

Before anyone is taken on as a supergrass, the police have to ask permission from the Crown Prosecution Service, and then strict procedures have to be followed.

In 1978, a special Police Protection Squad was set up to look after 'supergrasses' who, having appeared as key witnesses in criminal trials, had to be provided with new identities to safeguard their lives. The first such case was Derek Creighton 'Bertie' Smalls, an armed robber from north London who helped jail 27 bank robbers for a total of 315 years in a series of trials at the Old Bailey.

Since then, new identities have been granted in 170 cases – around 700 individuals when family members are included. The complexity and subterfuge involved are often not understood. Once a name has been selected, the cooperation of up to thirty organizations is needed to make a single new identity safe. Bogus documents must be obtained to cover educational qualifications, insurance, employment and medical histories, pension rights, bank accounts, mortgages and, in many cases, social security benefits.

Since the Police Protection Squad was set up, none of those given new identities has been harmed. Some have moved within the United Kingdom, but the danger to a significant proportion is so great that they have to be found new homes abroad, as far away as Australia and the United States.

If an informant, having given evidence, decides that he still wants to live on his old patch, despite police advice to the contrary, he is then on his own. No further protection can be forthcoming, even for those who have changed identity and moved home.

It was clear from the beginning that Donald Barrett was very anxious about what was going to happen to him: where could he now go in the system that was safe? He had served his previous sentence on the 'supergrass' wing at Bedford Prison. Having 'grassed' hardened criminals before, he would be in danger unless he was put in a protected wing again. Detective Superintendent MacRae recalls, 'It's clear that he'd be going to prison for a long time and it was possible that he'd be rubbing shoulders with the very people he'd given evidence against in the past. Those people would, without doubt, take his life. He could never live through a prison sentence. He wouldn't even get to trial.'

It was also of concern to Donald Barrett that, in the past, he had spoken at length to David Croke about his previous appearance for the Crown and his subsequent reduced prison sentence. Mr Croke asked many questions about how he was dealt with both before and after he turned supergrass. Mr Barrett was therefore desperate to get in first, before Mr Croke could volunteer, so he agreed to help and cooperate with the police straight away.

A statement was then taken from Mr Barrett in which he outlined the different cases he felt he could assist the police with. This covered a number of other robberies in which he had been involved. The statement was taken 'without prejudice', which means that he was not cautioned when he gave the information and it could not be used against him in court. It was just for background information.

This statement was then given to Detective Chief Superintendent Gwynn who had to go and see the Director of Public Prosecutions (DPP) to find out whether or not Donald Barrett would be allowed to become a supergrass. He met the Deputy DPP and another meeting was arranged for the following day, once all the papers had been read.

It is the responsibility of the DPP to grant anyone the status of resident informant, or supergrass, and, to help make this decision, a number of guidelines are laid down. The DPP must ask whether it is more in the public interest for one criminal to receive a full sentence or for a large group to be put away. This situation is still far from routine and each case has to be carefully considered on its own merits.

What made this case even more unusual was that never before had anyone been allowed to turn supergrass for a second time. Donald Barrett was given a reduced prison sentence back in 1980, when he turned supergrass and gave evidence against his co-accused in a case of armed robbery.

The Crown Prosecution Service, which is responsible for preparing serious criminal cases for trial, met with senior police officers to discuss the implications of Mr Barrett appearing for the Crown. One rule that must be strictly adhered to is that evidence given in such cases must be corroborated. This means that every time Mr Barrett implicated someone, his word alone would not stand up in court; there had to be supporting testimony.

It was a difficult time for the investigating team.

Nobody thought Mr Barrett would be granted permission a second time round to appear for the Crown. Mr Barrett was nervously awaiting the outcome at Milton Keynes police station. Detective Constable Kevin Shapland was one of the officers with him and he, too, felt that there was likely to be an unfavourable decision. He remembers, 'Barrett was desperate to know what was going to happen to him. If he didn't become a supergrass, then he would have to spend his time as a rule 43 prisoner. This means he would probably be placed in solitary confinement and the only people he would meet would be sex offenders. He really had no option but to go for resident informant; his future depended on it.'

The next day, after an intensive meeting between the DPP's office and the senior investigating officers, it was decided that Donald Barrett would be granted the status of resident informant. He therefore became the first man ever to turn supergrass for a second time.

Once the decision had been taken, Mr Barrett was moved from Milton Keynes to a secure police station in east London. A special incident room was set up and twelve detectives began to reinvestigate incidents, evidence and criminals that Mr Barrett was telling them about. He was interviewed daily by two officers, one of them Detective Constable Kevin Shapland: 'He had good days and bad days. He was prone to mood swings and was constantly worried about what was going to happen to him. He had a real presence about him and was like a caged tiger in many ways, but for all that, we were able to work effectively together over a long period of time.'

Even though Mr Barrett had been allowed once more to give evidence against his co-accused, there was no guarantee that he would receive a lighter sentence. It is up to the judge, on hearing the evidence, to decide on the sentence and, as this was going to be a test case, it was impossible for anyone to determine the outcome beforehand.

What quickly became apparent was the meticulous planning that had been necessary before any of these robberies were carried out. In one case, the preparation had taken a year to come to fruition.

It turned out that the Shields depot had, in fact, been the main target for a future robbery that needed careful planning and, as Alan Turner had only recently joined the company, the team were going to give it a few months before setting a final date for the raid.

Then, when Mr Turner discovered that he was going to be driving a security van carrying gold bullion, the gang, led by Mr Croke, decided that it would be an easy target. Mr Turner had driven this route once before and knew only a few days in advance that he would be making another trip. Plans had to be quickly prepared. This explains why Mr Barrett had already made holiday plans for the family. He was planning to rejoin them in Portugal the day after the robbery.

Mr Croke had asked Mr Barrett to fly back for the job, and it is somewhat ironic that, after all the careful planning involved with the other robberies, it was the desire to earn a quick buck that had let them down.

It seemed that David Croke was the brains behind the team. Mr Barrett had known him for about two years. They were mutual friends of George Ince, and it is likely that they were introduced by him. Mr Ince and Mr Barrett were the same age and both were well-known East End villains. They grew up together and, although Mr Barrett linked Mr Ince with several of the crimes that he had committed, the police were unable to find independent corroboration. As a result, Mr Ince was arrested, but later released and all charges against him dropped.

It seems that Mr Croke was quite happy to work with Mr Barrett even though he had turned supergrass once before. In fact, the team thought him safe. Detective Superintendent MacRae recalls, 'Imagine Donald Barrett carrying on with criminals, doing robberies, when they know he's a supergrass. It's staggering and astounding. What is clear is that there was a body of opinion among criminals that having once been a supergrass, he could never, ever, ever, be a supergrass again. They felt in this sense he was safer to indulge in criminality with than any other criminal.'

In the first few days following the arrests, the scene, the suspects and the vehicles used were examined. Searches were made of premises belonging to the suspects and evidence collated. Along with several others, Mr Barrett admitted the Armaguard robbery, which, he said, took a year to plan: 'On Wednesdays, Thursdays and Fridays, David Croke used to go out looking for security vans.... He saw an Armaguard vehicle doing a delivery and followed it back to the depot.... He realized it was a fairly small depot and he'd seen three or four security vans outside and wanted to know if there were any more inside, plus how many staff and a general idea of how they performed. He told me what he'd seen and the following morning I went there in a motor car with Dave in the boot with holes in for him to see what was going on. This was done for about six weeks.... During this time, we got to know the key-holders, Bill and Joe.'

The team researched Bill for several months. They found out where he lived, what shifts he worked and details about his family. Then, when they realized he had little children, they had to scrap everything: 'The main reason was because this had to be a sweet job and you simply can't wrap up kids. Dave said the only other way to do it was to plot up on the other key-holder, Joe, and that's what we did. Dave wanted to make up a completely new device so that there would be no connection with the other ones. He made up a plastic box with a switch on it which lit up a red light and made it look as if it was armed. It was, in fact, a dummy. We decided on the day, which was a Wednesday night in December 1985, and we met at Dave's bungalow.'

After the robbery, David Croke flew out to Malta, where he owned a flat. Mr Barrett told the police about a boat Croke had there that he named *Armag* after the robbery. The police flew to Malta and found the boat, which had been repainted and renamed. However, under ultra-violet light, the name *Armag* clearly appeared.

Detective Constable Kevin Shapland recalled, 'Once we checked out that this wasn't a local Maltese word, we knew we had excellent corroboration.'

Corroboration also came from forensic evidence. During the Armaguard robbery, a chain-link fence was cut within the perimeter of the premises, and when police searched Mr Croke's house, 'Emerald', some months later, they found a pair of wire cutters. These were taken for examination and cut marks on the actual wire matched the cutting edge of these wire cutters. Also, a balaclava was left at the scene and when Mr Barrett was arrested on the M1, he wore a wig, hairs from which matched fibres found on the balaclava.

The third member of the gang in the robbery, implicated by Mr Barrett, was a Glen Armsby who lived with Rita Croke's daughter. Mr Barrett told the police: 'Both Dave and Glen opened a number of accounts in building societies to put their share in, but, after coming back from Malta, Dave transferred his money to the Bank of Ireland because he said he was getting a better rate of interest there.'

Mr Barrett went on to give further details about Mr Croke's financial affairs, including the precise amounts each of them got when the proceeds were shared up. He said Mr Croke received £140 000 for the Armaguard job: 'I have been asked about a bank account held by Dave Croke at the Bank of Ireland, Seven Sisters Road.

The account was in the name of T. Moore.... I had some cheques from this account signed by Mr Croke in the name of T. Moore.'

Police recovered a briefcase from 'Emerald' that belonged to David Croke. It contained a great deal of correspondence with the names T. Moore and David Croke on it and, when police checked this with the bank, they saw evidence recorded in statements, paying-in slips and cheques that, again, corroborated everything Mr Barrett had said. From this wealth of information, police were able to prepare a graph of Mr Croke's finances and the sum of £140 000 appeared in his account shortly after the Armaguard robbery.

This revealed the very different ways that Mr Barrett and Mr Croke spent their money. Mr Croke was the investor, while Mr Barrett, who lived in a council-owned house, spent his share on holidays, clothes and expensive meals. He bought suits from Savile Row, and it was a standing joke among the police that he spent more on his tie and hankie than they did on an entire suit.

Mr Barrett admitted the robbery in Tottenham at the hops warehouse, where he again implicated Glen Armsby and David Croke: 'We saw the gateman arrive and, after about five or ten minutes, we went in.... Dave went into the tea room and laid out a mock-up bomb which he had made up. It consisted of a box with a strap and contained workings he'd bought from a model shop and a shotgun cartridge which had had the shot removed and cloth put in its place .... Two guards came into the office, which took us by surprise as on all the occasions we'd watched it, there had only been one. We took them both into the tea room where Dave showed one of the guards how the device worked by remote control. He then placed the cartridge on it and strapped it on to the spine of the older guard ... we made a cup of tea and told the guard to carry it back to the van .... As Dave was coming out of the van, the manager arrived in a

Vauxhall. I went over to him and told him to get out. He refused and so I fired a shot into the ground. Because of the noise, three people came out of the storage area. Glen went towards them and meanwhile I took the manager into the toilets. While I was there, I heard another gun go off, which I later discovered from Glen was his shotgun going off because he'd had it cocked. I came back out and Dave told us to go. He had put the money into the back of the gateman's car as we'd taken the keys from him earlier. Glen got in that car with Dave and I took the manager's car so I could block the road if anyone came after us. We went to the garages where the Marina was and transferred the money. Dave drove off in the Marina and Glen and I walked further down the road to where I had left my car. We then met back at Dave's house and shared the money out. We got £30 000 each and the bags containing the money were later burnt.'

After Mr Barrett had given details of where the gunshot was fired, police went to the scene and found the bullet hole. Again, the details of the money shared out was corroborated through Mr Croke's bank account.

In total, Mr Barrett admitted twenty-three offences. He gave information relating to crimes that had not been linked with those in custody, including robberies in Greenwich and Bristol. He was asked to describe scenes and events so that the investigators could attempt to identify areas of potential corroboration. Original investigation files were drawn and the original exhibits collected. The scenes were reinvestigated in the light of the new information. In some cases, the offences were three years old, but further searches and examinations were undertaken in an effort to link the scenes with the suspects. All the scenes had been examined for fingerprints, but no marks implicating other members of the team were found. Where Mr Barrett's evidence could be cor-

roborated, charges were made against the people implicated, but where evidence could not be corroborated, the
people involved were released without being charged.

Mr Barrett was interviewed for nearly nine months,
and then remanded in custody on a special supergrass
wing before the case finally came to court in April 1988.
Detective Constable Kevin Shapland was in regular contact with him: 'Over the months, I got to know Donald
Barrett very well and although he was a dangerous criminal I had a degree of professional regard for him. He
chain smoked, but drank very little. He was a Jekyll and
Hyde character: one side revealed the charming family
man who was kind and considerate, whilst the other
showed this incredibly ruthless man who would stop at
nothing for his gains.'

Mr Barrett was concerned about the first part of his
cross-examination in court because details of *his* past,
revealing the crimes he had committed, would come out.
He had fifteen previous convictions, the first of which
occurred when he was just twelve years old. As he grew
older, the crimes became more serious and some of his
previous convictions included: possessing firearms with
intent to commit robbery, wounding with intent and
assaults on the police. Many of his crimes were very serious indeed and he was rightly concerned that the court
might lack sympathy for him. During the trial, he was
escorted from his police cell by Detective Constable
Kevin Shapland, who remembered, 'He was very nervous for the first few days. His only concern was what
kind of sentence he would get. We had asked him to
confront David Croke and Glen Armsby before the trial,
because we felt it would help prepare him. In fact, he
spoke very well in court.'

David Croke refused to answer any questions regarding the charges against him. In fact, the only words he
said throughout interviews were, 'I want my solicitor to
be here', yet he pleaded guilty to nine offences because

of the strong evidence against him. These included the Tottenham, Armaguard and Shields robberies. He was sentenced to a total of twenty-three years.

Although Glen Armsby admitted the Tottenham robbery in interview, the police concentrated their efforts on getting a conviction for the most serious case – the Armaguard Robbery. For this, he was sentenced to a total of fifteen years' imprisonment. The files remain open on three offences that can be activated at any time with the permission of the court.

Alan Turner was sentenced to seven years and Rita Croke got a suspended sentence.

In this case, the legal system was on trial itself and some people took the view that Donald Barrett should have been put away for life, while others thought that this was not appropriate because it would not recognize the contribution he had made to a reduction in crime. He pleaded guilty to twenty-three offences.

Police officers went into the witness box to give an insight into the help Mr Barrett had given them, after which the judge mulled over the sentence for twenty-four hours. The next morning, he gave Donald Barrett sixteen years' imprisonment. This was reduced to twelve years on appeal – a sentence the police thought very fair. Mr Barrett served the first part of his sentence in the supergrass wing at Reading prison and, for the rest of his time, he will be placed in a protected prison wing.

When the trial was over, eight people received a total of seventy-one years' imprisonment, and the judge described some of the attacks as 'one step removed from terrorism'.

The hours of dedication put in by the whole inquiry team had finally paid off, and, for Detective Constable Kevin Shapland, it was a great personal success: 'All this came about because of one perceptive fourteen-year-old boy who, by a quirk of fate, had watched a video of *Crimewatch*. Without his information we would never have looked at that house in Broxbourne, and I have no doubt that this team would have carried on and committed many more major crimes.'

5

A CHAPTER OF REVELATIONS

When Ronald Harrison's body was discovered on Wednesday morning, 7 November 1990, it was at first thought that he had died from natural causes. He had been unwell for some time with Hepatitis B and had been forced to retire early from work as a result. However, when police officers arrived at the scene, his death was immediately treated as suspicious. There was blood on the pillow and scratch marks on his arms and legs. He looked like he had been tortured and, although the post mortem was not until the next day, the hunt for his murderer began immediately.

Ronald Snowden Harrison was born in Doncaster in 1938. He was a well-educated man, having attended Cambridge University where he obtained an MA (Hons) degree. He left the university in June 1962 and started teaching as assistant master at the John Lyon School, Harrow on the Hill, Middlesex. Known as Ron, he taught English and remained at the school until 1967, when he moved to Rickmansworth Grammar School, near Watford. Ron was a highly respected school teacher and, in 1971, he became deputy headmaster at Haberdashers' Aske's School for Boys in New Cross. Four years later, he moved to Wallington High School in Sutton, where he remained until he retired on medical grounds in April 1990.

In 1974, Ron bought a house in Plum Lane,

Plumstead, London SE18. It was a typical Victorian terraced house in need of repair. It had three bedrooms: a front bedroom, a second bedroom, used by Ron, and a third bedroom, which he used as an ironing room. Downstairs was a living room, a kitchen/diner and conservatory. The living room had a large front window and, instead of curtains, Ron had wooden shutters. He was rather proud of these and would always close them at night.

Ron was a sociable man. He had lots of friends, often hosted dinner parties and frequently went to the theatre. He was also deeply religious and attended the weekly service at St Paul's Church, Deptford. He had been worshipping there for many years.

Canon David Diamond was the parish priest and he had been there for over twenty years. He was extremely popular within the local community and had known Ron Harrison since the early seventies. They had met when Ron was at Haberdashers' Aske's. Canon Diamond used to visit the school and they became good friends.

The Sunday before his death, 4 November, Ron went to church as usual. He read the lesson, something he always did at this time of year because his birthday was on All Saints' Day, 1 November. Canon Diamond remembered how frail and fragile Ron looked. The previous evening, Ron had cooked a birthday dinner for a number of friends. They left around midnight and one of his closest friends, Roger, phoned him the next morning to offer him a lift to church, but Ron had already arranged for a taxi to collect him.

Three days later, at about 10 a.m. on Wednesday 7 November, Mrs Parker, a cleaner, went to Ron's house as usual. She had cleaned for Ron for eight years and, when she arrived that morning, she knocked on the door, but there was no reply, so she let herself in. The front door had two locks, a mortice and a Yale. Only the Yale was locked so she presumed Ron was inside as he always double-locked the front door when he went out.

She went into the living room and, seeing that the window shutters were still closed, opened them. She noticed that the sofa had been moved in front of the shutters, so she pushed it back to its normal position. She then set about doing her chores. The kitchen table needed clearing as what she assumed were the saucepans used for last night's dinner were still there.

Some time later, after she had finished the washing up and had still heard no sound from Ron, she went upstairs and knocked on his bedroom door. There was no reply. She opened the door, saw the curtains were still drawn and found Ron lying face down in his bed. There was blood on the pillow.

As she was wondering what to do, the telephone rang. She went downstairs to answer it. It was Roger, one of Ron's friends. She explained what had happened and Roger asked her to go back into the bedroom and check again on Ron while he waited on the phone. Mrs Parker went into Ron's bedroom and pulled back the quilt cover. She felt him and shook him. It was obvious that he was dead. She picked up the bedside phone and told Roger. He told her he would drive over straight away. Then she telephoned the police.

Detective Inspector Christopher Allen was having lunch with a colleague in Woolwich when his pager sounded; it was 1.20 p.m. The call was urgent and he left immediately. Half an hour later, he was in Plumstead talking to the uniformed officer outside Ron's house. He recalled, 'When I first walked into Ronald Harrison's bedroom, I felt something wasn't quite right. When we moved the body, we saw that there were scratch marks to his face and legs. Embedded in his right leg was a penny. It was a gruesome sight, and it looked like he had been tortured. I looked round the room and saw an empty credit card holder by his bed, yet there was a Barclaycard statement on the table with no sign of his card.'

As Ron had been ill for some time, both Roger and Mrs Parker told the police that they thought he had died from natural causes. However, Detective Inspector Christopher Allen instinctively felt that there was more to it. Only at a post mortem would it be possible to confirm exactly how Ron had died, and because this could not take place until the following day, Detective Inspector Allen decided that it was imperative to preserve the scene where the body had been found. He immediately stopped anyone else from entering the bedroom, or the house; if this was murder, he could not risk losing a single shred of evidence. He did not want to waste time, so he immediately called the scenes of crime officers to the house, and they began the task of searching for vital clues. Every inch had to be carefully examined.

Ron's body was taken away and both Mrs Parker and Roger were asked to make a statement. On the downstairs table, Detective Inspector Christopher Allen found a diary. It belonged to Ron and inside he had kept a meticulous record of things he had done and people he had met. Alongside the diary was a Barclaycard receipt for Sunday lunch, 4 November, and the amount paid was £68.

An incident room was set up and the next morning, at the post mortem, the pathologist confirmed the police's worst fear: Ron had been murdered. The pathologist explained that Ron had received heavy blows to his neck and there was bruising on his chest wall, which indicated that his attacker had been sitting or kneeling on his chest, leaning on his neck with his forearm. There were marks on Ron's chin that suggested he had tried to pull the arm of the attacker off him, and the pathologist thought there may well be scratches on the arm or the hand of the attacker. Ron's larynx had been torn and the cause of death was strangulation.

Once the police had official confirmation that they were, in fact, faced with a murder inquiry, a team was quickly assembled under the command of Superintendent Banks. Twenty-five officers were drafted on to the inquiry and Detective Inspector Christopher Allen was put in charge of the day-to-day running of the investigation. He held his first briefing later that day at Shooters Hill police station, south east London: 'I've just come back from the post mortem and I can tell you that Ronald Harrison was murdered in an extremely brutal fashion. The pathologist has told me that there's a strong possibility that two men were involved in the murder. I want you to bear in mind that, at the moment, the last sighting we have of Ron is on Sunday 4th November, and his body wasn't found until yesterday – Wednesday 7th November, so it's crucial we find out what he was doing between those dates. At the house I found Ron's diary, which is literally full of names, so I want a couple of officers to begin checking through those straight away.'

During the early stages of the inquiry, it quickly became apparent that Ron was gay. His diary revealed that he frequently visited gay pubs and clubs in London's West End, and that he sometimes picked up rent boys. It was crucial for the police to pursue this area of his life, but when they initially approached the gay community for information, they received a very negative response. This was due in part to an article that had appeared in a gay newspaper criticizing a murder investigation for misuse of information. In particular, they were worried that names would be stored on a computer. So, a great deal of time was spent trying to improve this relationship. A letter was written to the newspaper explaining how the information gained was going to be used and reassuring them that computers were not being used on this inquiry. A member of the

Gay London Policing Group went to the incident room at Shooters Hill to see for himself how the investigation was being run. Detective Inspector Christopher Allen recalls, 'It was a very difficult time for us. We desperately needed the help of the gay community, and an enormous amount of time was spent in building this relationship. I think it was a credit to us all that we did eventually manage to gain their trust. From this point onwards we began to get a much better response. We were able to build up a picture of Ron Harrison's behaviour in the West End.'

Police discovered that Ron was a very generous man. He often paid for lunches, drinks and dinner. He always had good wine in the house, and was more than happy to share it. When he met his pick-ups in the West End, he always paid the taxi fares back and forth to his home. Police spoke to literally dozens of people with whom Ron had worked and there was not the slightest hint of any untoward behaviour in this area of his life. He kept his gay life very much apart from his work, and the area where he lived. This probably explains why he preferred to take a taxi to the West End; it was easier to retain his anonymity.

The investigation team initially split into several groups: those checking the names of the gay people he met, others working at the house, hoping to find more clues, while Detective Sergeant Bernard Page and a number of officers toured the area where Ron lived, doing house-to-house enquiries.

They were desperate for someone to come forward who had seen Ron on the Monday. It was becoming more and more crucial to find out what he had been doing that day because, although his body was not discovered until Wednesday morning, the pathologist said that Ron had been dead for a maximum of seventy-two hours. This meant that he had either been murdered on Tuesday or, more probably, on Monday.

Unfortunately, when the local neighbourhood was questioned, detectives were inundated with information from people who said they had seen Ron alive on Monday, Tuesday and even Wednesday. It was, of course, impossible for all these people to be right. However, knowing which pieces of information to discard at this stage in the investigation was very difficult.

One neighbour said she had seen Ron getting into a taxi with two boys, while another said she thought it was with just *one* person. Albert and Kitty were Ron's next-door neighbours, and Kitty recalled that she went to bed just before midnight on Monday 5 November. When she was in bed, she heard a lot of scuffling next door and it seemed to be coming from Ron's bedroom. She heard three knocks and then a thud.

About the same time, Albert was in the garden, smoking his pipe. He noticed that Ron's bedroom light was on and that the curtains were closed. He saw the silhouette of a person move across the window. This was followed by a second silhouette, and it looked like the person was carrying something.

Kitty also noticed that on Tuesday lunchtime, Ron's bedroom curtains were still closed. She thought this very strange because he always opened them. It was something he was pedantic about.

This information immediately suggested that Ron had been murdered on the Monday night, as originally thought. However, the police needed more witnesses to come forward and were desperate for further sightings of Ron on Monday 5 November.

Meanwhile, officers searching the house had found several interesting items. Detective Sergeant Ron Turnbull saw a darning needle lying with the point upwards in Ron's bedroom. He remembers, 'We were conscious of the particular injuries on Harrison, and therefore were looking for something which could have caused them in the immediate vicinity of where he was found. Downstairs we found broken glass, shards of which again could have been used to cause these wounds.'

Downstairs, detectives also discovered traces of blood on the sofa in the lounge. Ron's own blood was compared and quickly eliminated. However, there was sufficient for a DNA probe to be done. This was a significant breakthrough and gave detectives a DNA profile of the possible killer of Ron Harrison. Inspector Christopher Allen recalls, 'This was a real bonus for us. We didn't have a name as yet, but it could prove useful for a future comparison. Unfortunately we had hundreds of people to talk to and it would take weeks to arrange blood tests for everyone. We had to narrow down the list first, and to do this we desperately needed more information.'

Ron's friend Roger had told police that the Sunday before he died Ron had arranged to meet a friend of his called Michael Slater for lunch. Michael was originally going to meet up with Ron at church and he was very distressed when Michael did not turn up.

Now, apart from the neighbours who had heard noises coming from Ron's bedroom, police had no positive sightings of Ron after church on that Sunday morning, 4 November. The Barclaycard receipt for Sunday lunch, which Detective Inspector Christopher Allen had found on the dining room table, confirmed that he was still alive then, and if Michael Slater had met him later that day, and accompanied him at lunch, then police were looking at someone, who, as far as they were concerned, was the last person to have seen Ron alive. Michael Slater therefore became the police's first real suspect.

Michael Slater was twenty-three years old and had attended Haberdashers' Aske's in New Cross. Ron Harrison had moved on before Michael started, but they were introduced through a mutual friend from the school many years later. When Michael left school, he went to Hatfield Polytechnic and studied mechanical engineering. He left in December 1983 and, early the following year, started work as a trainee accountant. He originally lived with his parents in south east London, but, in January 1985, he moved to live with his partner in Ilford.

During the past five years, Michael had met up with Ron on a regular basis, so police were anxious to speak to him to find out what had happened on that crucial Sunday. He was brought in to the police station to make a statement.

He began, 'We made arrangements to meet at St Paul's Church at 10.30 a.m. and, afterwards, we were going to go to the Spread Eagle pub in Greenwich for lunch, but the previous night I'd gone out drinking with my Dad and got drunk. I felt dreadful that morning and couldn't make it so I telephoned Ron about 9.30 a.m. and said I'd meet him at the restaurant. I cycled there and arrived about 1.15. Ron was already sitting at the table drinking bitter lemon. The meal was a treat for me. We've been there about two or three times over the last few years. I think Ron chose it because it was on his way home from church.'

The Spread Eagle is a very well to do French-style restaurant, and Ron was a regular visitor. It is about five miles from Plumstead and Ron had booked lunch that day for himself and Michael. The bill came to £68. Ron paid by Barclaycard and, afterwards, they got a taxi back to Plum Lane. Michael recalls: 'I remember we had to get a taxi big enough to get my bike in. We got back to the house at about 4 p.m. It was empty. We chatted for a while in the living room and I moved the sofa into a different position. I remember we opened another bottle of wine and I drank nearly all of it, then I fell asleep on the sofa. Ron went upstairs to rest. I remember hearing *Songs of Praise* on the telly. Then, at about 8 o'clock, the phone rang. Ron answered it. He chatted for only a few seconds and put the phone down. He told me it was Timmy wanting to come round. I knew Timmy from St Paul's and had seen him about five or six times before. Ron told him that he had visitors and he couldn't come. He said he didn't want him round because all he wanted was money.'

Michael told the police that there were no more phone calls that night. Ron said he was going to ring Roger later on, and Michael stayed the night in the front bedroom. He recalls, 'The room was as normal except that there were papers all over the floor. There was also money on the floor, which I thought was a bit odd. When Ron went into his bedroom, he closed the door. I left mine slightly open. I got up twice during the night because I felt thirsty. I drank some orange from a carton in the fridge. I also had a bit of beef. Ron got up twice as well because he put his light on, which woke me up. It hadn't been agreed that I would stay the night. I had planned to cycle back from the restaurant. Ron asked me to come back. The next morning, Ron got up about 8.30 a.m. He came to wake me, but I still felt like sleeping so pretended to be asleep. I heard him pottering about downstairs. Then I heard the morning service on the radio. After it ended, at 10 a.m. or 11 a.m., I got up.

'Nothing of a sexual nature happened between Ron and I that night. Ron and I were only ever friends. There was never anything sexual between us. I never fancied him, but I suppose he fancied me. We never lived together. We used to visit clubs and we talked a lot about our lives. We were good friends.'

So, now it seemed Michael was with Ron on that crucial Monday, the day police felt sure he was murdered. As Michael Slater carried on with his story, they grew more suspicious: 'We didn't have anything in to eat so went out to lunch. We took a taxi to the Earl of Chatham pub in Woolwich. Ron said he'd heard it did good food. I had a gin and tonic and Ron had orange juice. We put the drinks on a small table and then went to order some food. We both had lasagne and chips. When we returned to our table, there was an old man sitting there. The people at the next table had told him that someone was already sitting there but he took no notice. We had our meal with this man sitting opposite. He was reading a newspaper, I think it was *The Times*. He was drinking a pint of beer and had a packet of prawn cocktail Quavers, which I assumed he'd brought in with him. I remember thinking this was a bit of a cheek because the pub didn't sell crisps. Afterwards we went back to Plum Lane by bus.'

Michael said that they got back to Ron's house at about 2 p.m. Some time later, the phone rang and Ron asked him to answer it because he thought it might be Timmy again. Michael said Ron was out shopping and the caller put the phone down.

Michael said he left Ron's house between 3.30 p.m. and 4 p.m. on that Monday afternoon and cycled home. It took him about forty-five minutes. He never saw Ron again. He heard of his death from a mutual friend on the Thursday morning.

Police now had to check out every detail Michael Slater had told them. Would his story break? Could he be the killer? He certainly had ample opportunity to murder Ron, if that was his intent.

Five days after Ron's body had been found, Detective Constable John Judges was searching the house when he came across a letter. He recalls, 'I was very excited when I found this in Ron's house. It was an Access statement, addressed to a Timothy Kelly, for £500. To find an alien letter in the deceased's house, which had no obvious relevance, was a major clue. Who was Timothy Kelly and what had he been doing in Ron Harrison's house? I took the letter back to the office.'

Detective Constable John Judges immediately began to research Timothy Kelly. It transpired that he was nineteen years old and lived on a local council estate in Deptford. He had a minor conviction for criminal damage and this offence was committed with another man called Mark Dooley.

Police quickly discovered that Timothy Kelly and Mark Dooley spent a lot of time together. They had known each other from school days and neither had a job. Both went to St Paul's Church, Deptford, where they were altar boys. Mark Dooley was eighteen and lived with his mother on the same estate as Timothy Kelly.

Previously, police had spoken to Canon Diamond and discovered that some of the boys from the church had gone round to Ron's house to do jobs for him. Ron was very generous and gave large tips for helping with chores like the gardening or cleaning the car. However, this bill was for such a large amount of money that detectives needed to find out who had put it there and why. So, on 16 November, Timothy Kelly was brought in to the police station.

Detective Constable John Judges and Detective Sergeant Bernard Page interviewed him. He said, 'I have been unemployed for seven months. The only work I have had for any length of time is for Shields and Whittaker in Creekside, Deptford. I worked there for about two years as a trainee in steel fabrication, cutting and welding. While I was there, I was paid weekly by cheque. I opened a bank account at the Midland and was given an Access card on application. I used it on occasions, and was quite good with it at first, but I lost my job about twelve to eighteen months ago and started to run up debts. I currently owe just under £500.

'I first met Ron Harrison about two years ago. I met him through Father Diamond, my parish priest at St Paul's. I have been going to the church for the past five years. I have been an altar boy there on a few occasions. I met Ron Harrison when some boys came to London on an exchange. They were sent to various houses, and one

176

of these boys was to stay at Ron Harrison's house. I drove with Father Diamond, the boy, and my friend Mark Dooley to Ron's house. We stayed there, talking, for about half an hour and Ron mentioned the state of his garden. I said I would do it with Mark. Father Diamond said it was a good idea, and Ron said he would pay us for it.

'I phoned up about a couple of weeks later and Mark and I went round one Sunday afternoon. We worked for a couple of hours. Ron gave us some cans of drink, and between £20 and £30 to share. On future occasions I went to Plum Lane mainly on Sunday after church. I always went with Mark and I would always telephone Ron before I went there. I would never go without phoning. I would always confirm that he was in first, and we would never go if he had company. This went on for about two years. I realized Ron was homosexual so I would never go there alone, nor have I ever stayed the night there.

'The last time I saw Ron Harrison was when I went to his house with Mark some three to four weeks ago. I didn't do any gardening that day. I just sat downstairs on the settee drinking cans of Holsten Pils, and Mark drank Special Brew. Ron wasn't drinking. I had the letter from Access in my pocket. Ron mentioned that he wanted the place decorated, and the fact that I owed money came up. I took the letter, a final reminder, out of my pocket and showed it to Ron. Ron said if I did the work for him, he would pay the Access bill for me. Mark didn't say much at all. I usually did all the talking when I went there. After we discussed the decorating, Ron showed me the room he wanted doing up. It was a small room upstairs, and it had an ironing board and cupboard in it. I arranged to phone him later and, after about two hours, Mark and I left. I gave the Access letter to Ron and he left it on his dining room table, which he used as an office.'

On Sunday, 4 November, Timothy Kelly said he went to his sister's house during the day and, later that evening, he went to Father Diamond's house. He left about 11 p.m. and then returned to his sister's house to stay the night because she had a broken window, which was only covered with plastic sheeting, and he wanted to make sure she was all right.

The next day, Monday 5 November, he stayed at his sister's house all day. His cousin was also there. He went out to the phone box to telephone Ron. It was some time during the afternoon, between 2 and 2.30 p.m. He remembered that someone other than Ron answered the phone and, when Ron wasn't there, he put the phone down. He didn't ring back and he said that he never went to the house again. Then, at about 6 p.m., he went out with his cousin and Mark Dooley to the fireworks display at Deptford adventure playground. He left when it finished and went back to his sister's house where he again stayed the night.

So, it seemed that Timothy Kelly had the perfect story. He admitted making the phone call on Monday afternoon, which Michael Slater had already explained to the police. Father Diamond had said previously that Ron was known to pay over the odds for chores around the house, and it was quite normal for boys like Timothy Kelly to visit the house and help out.

However, Detective Sergeant Bernard Page, who was interviewing Timothy Kelly, felt that there was something not quite right about him. Although he seemed very confident and sure of himself throughout the interview, his attitude was very defensive: 'I felt that either he had previously had a bad experience with the police or he was guilty of something, and I became so uneasy that, before he left the police station, I asked to see his wrists. When he pulled up his sleeves, I saw distinctive scratch marks on both arms. Kelly said that he got them falling over drunk one night, but I felt they could have been defence wounds caused by some sort of struggle.'

So, now the police were looking at two strong suspects, but neither seemed to have a motive for the murder and, so far, there was no supporting evidence on either one of them. They decided to bring Mark Dooley in to the police station to find out if his account of the weekend's events matched that of Timothy Kelly.

The same officers, Detective Constable John Judges and Detective Sergeant Bernard Page, interviewed him. He said, 'I first met Tim Kelly when I was about eleven or twelve years old. We lived in the same area, and even worked together at Shields and Whittaker. For the past three to four years I have been going to St Paul's. Tim Kelly also goes to the same church. When I was younger, I was an altar boy at that church. I met Ron Harrison in the summer of 1989. I was introduced to him by Father Diamond one Sunday after mass.'

Mark Dooley went on to explain that he and Timothy Kelly had volunteered to do Ron's garden for him, for money, and that this had been going on now for some time. Like Timothy Kelly, he knew Ron was gay and would always telephone before going to the house. Mark Dooley said that Ron had asked them to do some decorating because, as winter was approaching, there was less to do in the garden.

The last time he had been at Ron Harrison's house was about five weeks ago. He went with Timothy Kelly. It was a Thursday afternoon and Ron's portable television was not working correctly, so they tried to tune it in for him. Ron then started talking about the decorating.

Mark Dooley said, 'We didn't do any work that day. Ron didn't even show us round the house. He told us first that he wanted the front room doing and then the hall. I have only been in the conservatory, the kitchen, the front room, the toilet, and the landing to the toilet. I have never been in any bedroom or other room upstairs. I've no reason to go there.'

He then went on to explain that on Monday 5 November, he had gone to a fireworks display at the adventure playground with Timothy Kelly and his cousin. They arrived around 7 p.m. and left about 10 p.m. He went home straight afterwards because he had to wake his brother up. He was due to start work at 10 p.m.

Before Mark Dooley left the police station, Detective Sergeant Bernard Page asked to look at his arms. He had cuts and scars on his wrist that he said he had got from falling outside a pub. Sergeant Page recalls, 'I found it extraordinary that Mark should have the same injuries and give the same explanation as Timothy Kelly, and I felt that they'd concocted a story between them. I didn't believe a word they were saying. It all sounded too good to be true, and I became even more suspicious of them both.'

There were also a number of important discrepancies in the boys' statements – notably details of how the decorating came to be mentioned by Ron, and the fact that Mark Dooley claims that they did not look round the house. He even went so far as to say that at no time did they go upstairs.

However, other than make the police even more suspicious of them, there was little more to go on. It certainly did not make them the murderers. In fact, a lot of what the boys said was true. Ron, in his retirement, was at times very lonely and he desperately sought companionship. He enjoyed the company of young men, and often bought drinks for them. Detectives felt he was an 'easy touch' for those who wanted to take advantage of him.

Ron continued to pay out frequently for booze, mostly gin. He had been drinking regularly before his death and, as his health gradually deteriorated, he sought solace, not only in the church, but through heavy bouts of drinking gin. Friends explained that, on many occasions, Ron went to bed drunk, unaware of who was still in the house or, indeed, what they were doing. It was at times like this that his property and money went missing.

After his retirement, Ron quickly realized that he was not as well off as he thought he was. Living only on his pension, the cash was beginning to run out. In fact, when detectives searched his house, they found a note in one of the bedrooms. It was written by Ron and listed his income. Alongside the figures were ways he might reduce his expenditure: 'no Margaret' suggested that he was considering giving up his cleaner, and 'no treats for the boys' suggested that he was no longer going to pay out money readily to the boys who mowed the lawn for him whenever they felt like it.

The two boys, Mark Dooley and Timothy Kelly, along with Michael Slater were so far the strongest suspects, but, as the inquiry moved into December, the police were little further forwards. Unfortunately, not enough clues or evidence emerged to pinpoint anyone. As far as they were aware, Michael Slater was the last person to have seen Ron alive, but they had been unable to break down any part of his story. The police felt sure that Mark Dooley and Timothy Kelly were lying, but they had nothing to prove this. What they feared most was that the murderer was still unknown to them, perhaps a casual pick-up from the West End.

Detective Inspector Christopher Allen recalls, 'I remember as it was coming closer to Christmas, we all felt very depressed. The team were divided on who they thought the killer was and why, but we didn't have enough evidence on any one person. Then, unfortunately, we suffered from our own success because we uncovered loads of possible suspects: the rent boys he'd picked up, his friends and acquaintances. Any one of them could be the killer. We were faced with a monumental task. Added to this I had to fight to keep all my officers. I'd already lost about ten to other inquiries and it was hard to justify having more staff when we weren't really getting anywhere. To be honest I was just hanging on, waiting to get a break.'

New clues were beginning to emerge from the murder scene. Two fingerprint experts spent a week at Ron's house and recovered *ninety-three* different sets of palm or fingerprints. Nineteen were on the wallpaper immediately above the bed. Everyone who knew Ron was asked to give their prints on the assurance that the records would be destroyed when the investigation was completed. Nobody refused. Police ended up with hundreds of different marks, and checking them took experts at Scotland Yard a full two months.

During this time, detectives started to look at other possible areas, which might uncover more clues. Ron had lost his driving licence and used public transport almost exclusively, so it was decided to interview all the bus drivers and taxi firms in the local area to see if anyone had any information regarding Ron after the Sunday night/Monday morning.

Detective Inspector Christopher Allen recalls, 'It was a bit like looking for a needle in a haystack, but at this stage we were absolutely stuck. We knew Ron travelled mostly by taxi, and in his wallet were a number of cards from local cab firms. At the outset we were looking at between fifteen and twenty taxi companies.'

Detective Constable Paul Harty was given the task of visiting every one. His off-duty days were cancelled and he began working round the clock. He asked every proprietor, first, if they remembered sending cabs to Ron's house and, then, second, he showed a picture of Ron to see if they, or their drivers, recognized him. It was a laborious job, but if he could find anyone who picked Ron up on those crucial days, he just might provide the vital piece of information they needed.

At the end of the first week, Detective Constable Paul Harty had looked through literally hundreds and hundreds of dockets, but, unfortunately, none were for Plum Lane. Then he went to Amber Cabs in Plumstead High Street. He spoke to the proprietor, who could not recall sending a taxi to Plum Lane. Paul looked through all the dockets for the relevant dates and, after about half an hour, his stomach turned as he found what he was looking for. He could not believe it as he pulled out a docket that had Ron Harrison's address on it: a fare was collected on Monday 5 November at 6.30 p.m. and the cabby's name was written by the side. This was an incredible stroke of luck.

The driver turned out to be a local cabby who had been driving for many years. He remembered Ron Harrison and said that he had collected him on previous occasions. The first time he met him was about twelve months ago, although, up until now, he had not known his name.

He recalled that on Monday evening, 5 November, he was in the cab office when the request came in for a car to go to Plum Lane. It was about 6.30 p.m. He was the only driver available at the time, so he took the call. He set off immediately and, because it was only a mile and a half away, he arrived about ten minutes later.

He did not go to the front door, but sounded his horn outside. The downstairs front window light was on and the shutters were closed. After a few minutes, a boy, who looked about seventeen, came out of the house and walked down the garden path towards the car. He shouted and said he would be a couple of minutes.

A short time later, Ron Harrison came out of the house and stumbled his way along the garden path towards the gate; he was very drunk. Then, the boy who had originally come out of the house appeared again, only this time he was with another youth who was slightly shorter. They got into the back of the cab.

The taller one sat behind the passenger seat and the other behind the driver. Ron had gone back into the house to get something and they waited outside. After a few minutes, the taller youth became impatient and got out of the car. He shouted towards the house, but there was no sign of Ron. Then, as he got back into the car, Ron appeared. He shuffled across the road and got into the passenger seat.

Ron said he wanted to go to Barclays in Woolwich. He wanted the taxi driver to wait for him and then bring him back. During the journey, Ron kept trying to give directions. His voice was slurred and he smelt of either gin or vodka.

There was little conversation in the car and, when the taxi pulled up, Ron got out alone. He had to lean against the railings to help him keep his balance. The cash machine was about eight feet away. There was a blonde-haired lady using the first one, so he had to walk past her to the second machine. He had difficulty putting his card in, and the boys in the taxi were laughing at him. After about five minutes, he came back to the cab. He had been unable to withdraw any money from the machine and, on the return journey, there was silence in the car.

Ron Harrison paid the £4 fare. He gave the driver a brand new £10 note and asked for £5 change. He then walked towards his front door and the taxi drove off.

This information was crucial for the police: it pinpointed two youths. The police now knew that Ron was alive on the Monday evening after Michael Slater had left him, and attention focused on finding out who the two youths were.

Detective Inspector Christopher Allen recalls, 'This information from the taxi driver was a real breakthrough, particularly when we put it together with the evidence of Ron's next-door neighbours who had heard banging noises and seen figures in Ron's bedroom on the same night. We began to feel reasonably sure that the murder had been committed on that Monday night, and we could now almost certainly eliminate Michael Slater.'

The police knew that Ron had at least £5 in his wallet that evening, given to him by the taxi driver, but when the body was discovered, his wallet was lying on the table empty. Now that the police knew for certain money had been stolen, it gave them robbery as a possible motive. However, if this was the case, then it was likely something else had gone missing from the house. A thorough search began and, in a cupboard, the police found an empty box for a new portable television, along with two receipts for two televisions. Neither set was in the house. One was for a Philips and the other was for a Decca. Both had been bought from Rumbelows in Woolwich.

The manager of this branch of Rumbelows was able to confirm that Ron had bought the Philips portable on 8 September, paying by Visa, and that he had returned to the store on 13 October when he bought the Decca, again paying by Visa card.

The morale in the incident room was at an all-time high as new information was beginning to emerge. Those investigating the fingerprints had managed to identify several marks. A number were from gay partners whom the police had already eliminated. There were, however, other prints on the wall above the bed that the police were very interested in.

They gave the impression that someone had leaned against the wall while dragging something heavy on to the bed and they belonged to Mark Dooley. For someone who had repeatedly denied ever going into Ron Harrison's bedroom, he now had quite a lot of explaining to do.

As detectives went through the events of Monday 5 November once again, Mark Dooley stuck to his story of visiting the fireworks display with Timothy Kelly and his cousin. He said he saw several people there he knew and returned home about 10 p.m. He woke his brother up, who was going to work, and then he went out to buy some cigarettes. After this, he returned home. Mark Dooley was very calm and did not appear agitated or nervous.

The police had taken statements from other witnesses who said that Mark Dooley had gone to Timothy Kelly's house after the fireworks display, and not straight home. They contradicted Mark Dooley's version of events, but each time he was fed information, he gave a plausible reply. He claimed that it was some time ago and he could not remember exactly what had happened.

Detectives then began questioning him about Ron Harrison, in particular the rooms of the house that Dooley had been in:

'Kitchen, front room, toilet and hallway.'
'Have you ever been in his bedroom?'
'No, of course I ain't.'
'Is there any chance that you were in his bedroom for any reason whatsoever?'
'No. None at all.'
'Look, an awful lot of people are homosexual.'
'Well, I'm not.'
'Look, Mark, I've got to put it to you that I have irrefutable proof that you have been into that bedroom.'
'And I'm denying it.'
'Are you sure?'
'Well he might have said one day to go and get something. Yeah, it was probably an extension lead for the lawn mower.'
'Where was that kept?'
'As you walk in, there's a wardrobe. It was on there.'

Mark Dooley was becoming more and more agitated and nervous in his responses. He was obviously lying about going into Ron's bedroom, so, at this point, detectives halted the interview and formally arrested Mark Dooley for the murder of Ronald Harrison. His solicitor was called to the police station.

The interview recommenced an hour and a half later. Mark Dooley was asked if he had killed Ron Harrison. He replied, 'No.' He was also asked whether or not he was in a cab with another youth on Monday evening. Again, he replied, 'No.'

Detectives then told Mark Dooley that fingerprints had been found on the wall behind Ron Harrison's bed, nowhere near the wardrobe to which he had referred earlier, and that these prints corresponded with someone appearing to pull someone on to the bed. Mark Dooley replied:

'Well, when I went to get the extension lead I must have brushed against the wall.'
'The wardrobe is nowhere near the wall. The reason your fingerprints are on that wall is because you murdered Ron Harrison.'
'No. I never killed anyone.'
'Well, how come your prints are on the wall?'
'I fell against the wall and put my hand there to stop me from falling over.'
'How come you never mentioned that before?'
'I forgot.'
'How did you fall against it?'
'I tripped. There was a shoe on the floor and I tripped on the shoe.'
'Where was the shoe?'
'In between the bed and the wall.'

Detectives then went on to question him about another fingerprint found in one of the other bedrooms. He could give no explanation for this. Detective Sergeant Bernard Page remembers, 'Dooley was obviously very shaken. He was nervous and kept shivering. He kept fidgeting and tapping his foot. We had to tell him to stop because we thought it might interfere with the tape recording. After speaking to his solicitor, he appeared more composed. At the end of the interview we felt that we didn't have sufficient evidence to charge him, so he was released.'

Timothy Kelly was also brought in for further questioning. Detectives asked him whether or not he used an extension lead when doing the gardening. He said, 'Yes,' and explained that it was kept in the conservatory. He knew exactly where it was because *all* the gardening equipment was kept there. He went on to answer further questions about his and Mark Dooley's whereabouts on bonfire night. His story remained the same as before, and he said Mark had gone with him to the fireworks display. He admitted telephoning Ron on the Monday afternoon, but denied telephoning him on the Sunday.

Timothy Kelly was finally asked whether or not he would be prepared to stand on an identification parade at some future date. This he agreed to.

Detective Constable John Judges remembers, 'Kelly was very different to Dooley. He was so much more together. He appeared smooth and angelic, but underneath he was very calculating. I knew he was lying, but we still didn't have enough evidence to charge either of them.'

So, once again, it seemed that the police had hit a brick wall. Mark Dooley and Timothy Kelly were plainly lying, but that did not mean they were the killers. Perhaps the investigation team were looking at the wrong people after all, and the murderer was still unknown to them.

Detectives checking on the two television sets that were missing from Ron's house had come up with another name. In Ron's diary by the date 10 October, was the entry, 'Ronnie Vincent, TV stolen plus £30'.

Ronnie Vincent was twenty-three and unemployed. He had known Ron Harrison for about ten years. He was arrested on suspicion of burglary and brought in to the police station.

Ronnie said that when he was younger he used to go round and wash Ron's car. Ron started giving him booze and cigarettes. He admitted Ron was a soft touch, saying that he used to leave his wallet lying around and it was easy to take money out of it. Ron did not seem to mind because he never used to mention it.

Ronnie admitted taking the television set: 'Well, I did nick it. I went down there and I didn't have any money so I thought I'd get some off Ron. It was about three months ago. He went down the shops and I nicked the telly. I sold it to some geezer in the pub for £50.'

Unfortunately, Ronnie could not remember which television set he had stolen. Detectives believed his story, and he was never a suspect for the murder. What they now had to do was try to trace *both* missing sets.

The best way to do this was to make a national appeal, so, ten weeks into the inquiry, on 17 January 1991, an item was broadcast on *Crimewatch UK*. Unfortunately, it was the day war broke out in the Gulf and, because the news was extended, *Crimewatch* was switched to BBC 2.

Detective Inspector Christopher Allen remembers, 'We began to feel almost as if the fates were stacked against us, and I remember the feeling of disappointment when we were told that we were being moved from BBC 1. Everyone was very apologetic and, of course, we understood, but I remember saying to one of my detectives, "Who on earth is going to watch *Crimewatch* on the day war broke out in the Gulf?"'

Even so, three and a half million people watched the programme, but this was barely a quarter of the normal *Crimewatch* audience. Details of the missing television sets, along with their serial numbers, were put up on the screen. Nine calls came in to the studio concerning them and four were received back at the incident room. It was a disappointing result.

The next day, all the phone calls were followed up,

but, unfortunately, nothing came from them. The police had little more to go on.

Mark Dooley and Timothy Kelly were still strong suspects and so it was decided to hold an identification parade. Three witnesses said that they had seen Ron Harrison with the two boys on Monday 5 November. If the police could prove that these were Timothy Kelly and Mark Dooley, it would once again highlight the lies they continually told and strengthen the case against them. A week after the *Crimewatch* programme, Wednesday 23 January 1991, an identification parade was held at Brixton police station.

The first witness, a neighbour, walked along the line and failed to pick out either suspect. The second neighbour stopped and looked at Timothy Kelly standing at number seven and said, 'Yes, there's something familiar about number seven, but I couldn't positively say it was him.'

Finally came the taxi driver who had picked up the two boys with Ron on the Monday night. He had seen one of the boys in his mirror, and police were desperately hoping he would make a positive identification. As he walked along the line, they waited on tenterhooks. He was asked whether he recognized anyone and he said, 'No, I can't identify any of them.'

Detective Inspector Christopher Allen recalls, 'This was really agonizing. One witness had actually picked out Kelly, but she was so uncertain, that this couldn't be used in evidence. Our best bet was the taxi driver and when he failed to recognize either suspect, we were very disappointed. As we left, I remember Timothy Kelly saying, "Better luck next time" with a big smirk all over his face. A couple of officers and myself went round the corner for a beer. I began to feel that the inquiry was going to collapse into nothing.'

Still, the two boys could not be eliminated from the inquiry and a detective was sent round to check out their alibi. Detective Constable John Judges went to visit Richard MacVicar, the senior leader of the Deptford adventure playground who put on the fireworks display. He said he knew Timothy Kelly, but could not be sure whether he would recognize Mark Dooley. However, on that particular evening there had been over a thousand people at the display, and he had no idea if they had been there or not. He said the bonfire was lit at 7.30 p.m. and the fireworks display commenced at 8.20 p.m. and finished at 9 p.m. By 9.30 p.m. the bonfire had been doused and the area was clear.

Detectives went on to question a number of people whom Mark Dooley and Timothy Kelly claimed to have seen at the display. It seems that everyone missed them except Kelly's cousin, Angela. She insisted that they were there.

It was a long, laborious task and it still did not provide the vital break that they needed. Then, ten days after *Crimewatch*, Chief Superintendent Tony Humber received an urgent phone call from Canon David Diamond requesting to see him. Chief Superintendent Tony Humber was unconnected with the murder investigation, but a member of St Paul's congregation.

It was a Saturday morning when Chief Superintendent Tony Humber arrived at the church, and Canon Diamond was in rather a state. He explained that he had come across some information regarding the Ron Harrison murder and it affected two boys from the church. He did not know what to do. Chief Superintendent Tony Humber said that he must tell him everything and then he might be able to help.

Canon Diamond recalled that on Wednesday 23 January at about twelve noon he was walking along Deptford High Street when a woman he knew stopped to talk to him. She said that she had a friend who last week had watched *Crimewatch UK*, and a television set she had recently acquired was the same type as that mentioned on the programme. She then checked the serial number and it matched that on the screen. She was very worried and did not know what to do. The woman asked Canon Diamond what she should tell her friend. He told her he would think about it and contact her later in the day. From the description given of the boy who sold her the set, he felt sure it was Timothy Kelly.

Around 1 p.m. that same day, Timothy Kelly rang Canon Diamond to ask if he could have a lift to Brixton police station. It was the day of the identification parade. Father Diamond explained that, unfortunately, he had a funeral to take that afternoon. However, he wanted to see him on a very urgent matter. Timothy Kelly said that he would come round.

Almost immediately, Timothy Kelly arrived on the doorstep. When asked about the television set, he said that he had stolen it from Ron Harrison and then sold it on. He was, however, anxious to get to Brixton, so Canon Diamond gave him £10 for the taxi fare and arranged to meet him later that evening.

Around 6.30 p.m. Timothy Kelly and Mark Dooley went round to Canon Diamond's house. They explained that they had told the police that the last time they saw Ron Harrison was several weeks ago, but in fact, they had seen him on Sunday 4 November. They had deliberately told this lie because they felt it was too close to the murder for comfort.

They said that they had arrived at Ron's some time in the afternoon. He was on his own and very drunk. Timothy explained that he asked Ron about doing the decorating to pay off his Access bill. Ron replied that he wanted more than just that for paying the bill. He then made an indecent suggestion to him and, when this was rejected, he staggered upstairs to bed. So, out of spite, he and Mark stole the television. They had intended to take it back on the Monday, but when they telephoned, someone else answered and they just decided to keep it.

When Chief Superintendent Tony Humber heard the story, he knew that the murder investigation team had to be told immediately. Canon Diamond requested that the boys meet the police in the church. Inspector Christopher Allen remembers, 'At last we had the breakthrough, but I was terribly disappointed Canon Diamond hadn't come to see me sooner. Had we been able to confront Dooley and Kelly with this information, then I feel sure they would have confessed. Instead, by talking to them himself, Father Diamond had forewarned Dooley and Kelly and given them time to make up a story.' However, the police could see that at least part of the boys' story was now a lie. Timothy Kelly and Mark Dooley said they had stolen the television set from Ron Harrison on Sunday evening. They knew from Michael Slater's evidence that this simply was not true.

Inspector Christopher Allen agreed to meet the boys in the church at 4 p.m. on Wednesday 30 January. If they repeated the same story as they had told Canon Diamond, then they were going to be arrested for murder.

In view of the fact that this meeting was to be with him alone, Detective Inspector Christopher Allen was equipped with a concealed tape recorder. A number of officers were positioned around the church in case the boys tried to escape. At the beginning, both boys were cautioned. They admitted stealing the television, but maintained it had been on the Sunday. They said they had gone to Plum Lane around 6 p.m. Ron smelt strongly of gin. They then discussed payment of Timothy Kelly's Access bill and Ron made a sexual advance to Kelly. Ron then went to bed and, out of spite, they stole the television set that was on top of the large TV.

They claimed that on Monday 5 November, they telephoned to make arrangements to return the set, but as someone else answered they decided to keep it. The following day, they saw someone they knew in the street and asked her if she wanted to buy it. She agreed and they sold it to her for £50.

The meeting finished at 4.45 p.m. and Detective Inspector Christopher Allen immediately arrested them both for the murder of Ron Harrison. They were taken to Woolwich police station. Inspector Allen remembers, 'I don't think they could quite believe it. Kelly momentarily looked shaken, but he quickly recovered his composure and was soon back to his cocky, arrogant self. I think that after the identification parade they really thought they had got away with it. What we now needed was to speak to the woman who had bought the television set from Kelly.'

Jean had lived in Deptford for the past ten years and recently moved house, on 11 November. She had known Timothy Kelly for about eight years; he went to the same school as her son. She did not know his surname or exactly where he lived.

One evening at the beginning of November she recalled Timothy Kelly arriving at her house saying he needed some pocket money. He asked her if she wanted to buy a portable television set. It was in a black plastic bag and she thought it would be a good idea for the caravan. He said it was £50, so she agreed straight away, but, unfortunately, only had £40 in her purse, so borrowed £10 from a neighbour. She thought no more about it until she saw *Crimewatch UK*.

She recognized Ron Harrison's picture when it was shown on the programme. Father Diamond had performed her marriage ceremony some three years ago and he had taken Ron Harrison to the reception with him. Because of this, she watched the item with added interest. When the television sets were shown, she recognized the Decca as being the same one she had purchased from Timothy. She did not know what to do. She could not believe that he had committed murder, so she did not tell the police. Instead, she contacted an ex-neighbour and it was this neighbour who told Canon Diamond.

At 9 p.m., in an interview room at Woolwich police station, Detective Inspector Christopher Allen began questioning Timothy Kelly for the final time:

'This television set. Why didn't you tell my officers before how you came into possession of it?'
'No comment.'
'Are you going to answer any of these questions?'
'No comment.'
'Is the reason you're not answering the questions because you have finally been arrested for the murder of Ron Harrison and you've effectively run out of ideas?'
'No comment.'
'We can prove that you weren't there on Sunday.'
'No comment.'

Timothy Kelly refused to answer any questions regarding the stolen television set or his whereabouts on Sunday 4 November.

Meanwhile, Mark Dooley was being interviewed by Sergeant Bernard Page at Greenwich police station.

'You admitted to Mr Allen that you stole a television set from Ron Harrison's house on Sunday 4 November.'
'Yeah.'
'Are you positive it was on the Sunday?'
'Yeah.'
'Why are you so positive?'
'Because I remember exactly where I was on Monday and I know where I was on Sunday.'
'Where were you on the Monday?'
'With Timmy Kelly at the adventure playground fireworks display in Deptford.'
'That was in the evening.'
'All day long I was with Timmy in his sister's house.'
'I put it to you, Mark, that people you said were at the

fireworks display have got no recollection of seeing you there.'

'I wasn't with them at the fireworks display.'

'I'm not saying you were with them, but they were there and said they didn't see you or Kelly there.'

'So, there was another 150 people there.'

'Right. I understand from your previous interviews that you said you went upstairs into Ron Harrison's bedroom to look for an extension lead.'

'Yes.'

'Tell me exactly where in the bedroom you went.'

'By the bedside cabinet.'

'Now, can you explain how your fingerprints got on the wall?'

'I can't remember exactly how me hands got on the wall. I mucked about in the room a bit, then I pulled the bed out and there was this clock radio thing underneath the bed, like, which I wanted to have a look at.'

'And this story about the extension lead, that's all rubbish is it?'

'There was an extension lead there.'

'But you weren't looking for an extension lead?'

'No.'

'And what about this tripping over a shoe? Was that rubbish as well?'

'I have tripped over shoes before.'

'Did you trip over a shoe in his bedroom?'

'No.'

'So you've come out with a total pack of lies.'

'Not a total pack.'

'Well, did you trip over a shoe or not?'

'No.'

Detective Constable John Judges recalled, 'Mark Dooley was very streetwise. He lived by his wits, but unfortunately he had a loose tongue. He dug holes for himself which he found almost impossible to get out of. This was a major part of his downfall. In his final interview he went to pieces. He was very nervous.'

At the end of the interview, both boys were charged with the murder. Detective Inspector Christopher Allen recalls, 'We had the defence marks to both boys' wrists. They had lied endlessly about their alibis, their visits to Ron Harrison's house, and where they had been in his house. As well as Mark Dooley's prints, scientists also found a fingerprint belonging to Kelly in Harrison's bedroom. Finally, the blood found on the downstairs sofa was positively identified as belonging to Mark Dooley. We felt certain they had done it.'

Although the evidence against the two defendants was purely circumstantial, detectives felt that they had enough to put before a jury. During the investigation they had uncovered glaring discrepancies between statements provided by witnesses, and interviews conducted with Kelly and Dooley, particularly concerning the events of Sunday 4 and Monday 5 November:

- Michael Slater clearly stated that he was with Ron on Sunday evening and the police found two witnesses who had spoken to Ron on the telephone that evening, both saying that Ron mentioned to them that Michael Slater was at the house but made no mention of the defendants being there

- only when details of the stolen TV came to light did the boys admit to being with the deceased the day before the murder

- the defendants' claim that they stole the portable television from on top of the large TV in the living room – photographs of the room show quite clearly *ornaments* on top of the large TV, so how could they possibly be there if the portable was in that position on Sunday night?

- Mark Dooley only admitted going into the bedroom

when he was first confronted with fingerprint evidence, and at this interview it was not revealed to him that the police had actually found *five* sets of his prints on the wall above the bed – his first explanation could only account for two so, once again, his story changed

■ the crux of the defendants' alibi hinged on the supposed visit to the fireworks display, but again, there were many discrepancies regarding the time they left, who they went with and who they saw there, and it seemed that everyone, except Kelly's cousin, missed them.

Detective Inspector Christopher Allen was fully aware of the difficulties surrounding the prosecution case, which is always harder and much less conclusive when there are no actual witnesses to the murder or forensic evidence directly linking the murderer to the crime, as in the case of DNA.

He felt that Timothy Kelly certainly had a strong enough motive for killing Ron: 'He desperately needed money, and quickly. Ron was his only hope of short-term financial salvation. As Ron was becoming strapped for cash, he was less willing to pay out and this was irritating the boys. Dooley, for his part, was both workshy and easily led by Kelly. I think he saw in the situation some money easily obtainable for himself. We spoke to a number of people who said that Ron began to regard these boys as financial pests and, in fact, he was beginning to get frightened of them.'

The night Ron died, when he tried to get money from the cash dispenser, he failed to put in the correct PIN number. This possibly aggravated the boys further, hence the physical abuse of Ron. Police felt certain that the killing did not occur on the bed and that Ron was put into bed with the quilt cover on top of him, to try to hide the crime.

On 6 January 1992, Mark Dooley and Timothy Kelly appeared at the Old Bailey, charged with the murder of Ronald Harrison. Both pleaded not guilty. Three weeks into the trial, they pleaded guilty to manslaughter. Mark Dooley, who was seventeen when the offence was committed, was sentenced to seven years in a young offenders' institution. Timothy Kelly, who was twenty, was sentenced to eight years' imprisonment.

The investigation team were very pleased with the outcome of the trial. It had been a long haul, and there were times when it had looked like the case was never going to be solved. Detective Inspector Christopher Allen praised the work of all the team who had been involved in investigating such a cross-section of society: 'I suppose it was a classic who-done-it, which required a lot of quite dogged police work. Like everyone, you need a stroke of luck, and, I have to say, I was amazed when it came from the *Crimewatch* programme, especially in view of the fact that we had so few calls on the night and nothing had come from them. I think it was the sheer complexity of the victim and his lifestyle, alongside the lack of clues, which made it so difficult for us.'

The judge commended Detective Inspector Allen, his investigation team and *Crimewatch UK* for their crucial part in helping to solve this murder.

6

DOUBLE IDENTITY

'It went on throughout the night. The gun was put beside my ear, in my groin, and in my stomach. They told me exactly where my children went to school, their movements and my movements, and that if I was foolish enough to go to the police then they had plenty of friends who would send a little explosive parcel through the post. In between all these threats, there was the constant reminder that they were going to take my family away from me, and that I may never see them again, and that it would be my responsibility.'

These are the words of Andy Andrews, a father, who, along with his wife and two children, was held at gun-point for nearly fifteen hours.

Terry Allen, as we shall call him, was born in 1964, and had lived in Ipswich, Suffolk, all his life. He was unemployed and desperately short of money. He had been a small-time crook for many years – stealing had become a way of life, and the means of providing for his wife and two young children. Terry was desperate to hit the big time and, one day, when he met up with a life-long family friend, he thought he had found the answer to all his dreams.

Jack Marsh was seventy. He walked with a stick and wore a hearing aid. He was balding with a nervous tic in his left eye, and had been in trouble with the police many times before. Jack had been friendly with Terry's father for years, but, recently, he had become closer to Terry, visiting him several times a week. Jack's wife had died two years before, and he was lonely, seeking companionship. Terry looked up to Jack and they spent hours talking together about his past crimes.

Around the end of September 1990, Jack rang Terry and said that an old friend of his had asked him if he knew anyone who wanted to do a bit of 'business'. The man asking was German and, from the conversation, Terry gleaned that he was a criminal of some class who might have work. Terry needed the money, so agreed to a meeting. About an hour or so later, Jack picked him up and they drove to a pub in Ipswich.

When Terry first met John, he was standing at the bar. When he spoke, he had a foreign accent, German or Dutch. He gave Jack some tokens to play the fruit machine and then the two of them sat down. Terry recalls, 'John asked me about myself, in particular about the types of crimes I had committed and the kind of prison sentences I had served. I told him I'd only been in detention centres for three to four months, and he seemed surprised. He said I wasn't the type of person that he was looking for, but that he may be able to put a few things my way. He wrote down my telephone number in code in a small, dark-coloured book. He then looked at a mirror on the bar wall which said "Tolly Cobbold", and he said that if he called me he would use the word "Tolly". He then spoke to me about the type of crimes he had committed. He said he was only interested in crimes where he could steal at least £100 000. He said that he and his gang had been planning a job for some time which was likely to come off in the near future. He said all his jobs were thoroughly well planned, and he finished by saying that he fancied doing Tesco's supermarket in Ipswich and that I might be able to help.'

Terry was impressed with John; he liked him. John

was over six feet tall, in his late thirties, with mousy, short, straight hair. He was athletically built and spoke of his love of mountaineering. While in the pub, he constantly played with his fingernails, cleaning them with his lock knife. He smoked hand-rolled Golden Virginia cigarettes. Terry had never met anyone like this before; he really thought he was in with the big boys now and was going to go up in the world.

On the way back home, Terry asked Jack what he had thought John wanted him to do. Jack had no idea, but said to let him know if John rang.

Terry did not think that John was very impressed with him. However, a few weeks later, the phone rang and it was John. Terry immediately recognized his thick foreign accent. John asked Terry to find out the name of the manager at Tesco's and the type of car he drove. Terry still did not know what the job was; he thought perhaps they were going to rob a security van when it made its delivery. He did not know what to make of John's request, so telephoned Jack. Jack agreed to help him.

The two men drove to Tesco's superstore and sat in the car park. They identified the manager and saw him get into a red Rover. They wrote down the registration number and then tried to follow him, but he drove too quickly and they lost him as he was heading off towards Colchester.

John rang and said he was coming down. Jack agreed to collect him and bring him to Terry's house. When the three men met, Terry gave John a piece of paper that had on it the registration number of the red Rover. John was impressed and, when Terry made the coffee, John explained how he hated 'grasses', and how one such person had had acid poured on his face. The atmosphere suddenly turned sour.

Terry was worried; the conversation was aimed at him, and he was left under no illusions as to what would happen to him if he spoke to the police. Terry was frightened, not only for himself, but for his whole family. He contemplated pulling out, but felt it was impossible at this stage. John knew where he lived, he had seen photographs of his wife and young children; it was too late. He had to go along with whatever John wanted as he was already in too deep.

Some time later, John made contact once again and said he would be arriving with some other people. Terry telephoned Jack, but John had already said that he did not want Jack involved any more. Terry sent his wife and children out for the afternoon.

John arrived at Terry's house alone and, shortly afterwards, another man appeared. He was slim with short, dark hair and in his late twenties. The men spoke to each other, but no names were mentioned. The dark-haired man said he was unhappy about the view into the kitchen from the front window so Terry suggested that they move into the living room. They closed the curtains and watched some videos. It seemed that they were killing time. John drank coffee and the other man had tea. Nothing was said or discussed about Tesco's, then, around 3 p.m. the two men left.

Terry assumed that they were going to follow the manager home. He went to the window and saw John get into a gold-coloured four-wheel drive vehicle while the other man drove a red XR2.

Later in the day, John called to say that they had had no luck and he would have to bring a third man down. Terry assumed that they had failed in their attempt to follow the Tesco's manager home.

A few weeks later, Terry had arranged for his family to go out and, at about 1 p.m. there was a knock at the door. Standing in front of him were two men: one was the dark-haired man, but the other he had never seen before. There were no introductions – the men walked straight past him, through the hallway, and into the living room.

The third man was in his mid twenties, about five feet six inches and quite stocky. He had light-coloured hair, which was short and receding. He had a round face and spoke quietly with an Essex accent. The two men waited for about half an hour for John to arrive, then Terry made them all drinks and they watched videos before leaving around 3 p.m. They never explained what they were doing or where they were going.

A few days later, John spoke to Terry and asked him to look for a place to hide a car. They arranged to meet, and John suddenly turned to Terry and said, 'I need a car. Steal me a car. It must be quick, modern and have four doors.' Terry was frightened and explained that he had never done anything like this before: 'I was so frightened that for the next few nights I actually started to go out and look for a car to steal, but I didn't know how to do it. In the end I gave up trying. John kept ringing me and each time I put him off with excuses. I told him things like the alarm had gone off or I had been disturbed, but he continued to demand that the car be stolen. He told me that time was running out.'

After weeks of hesitation during July 1991, Terry finally got a car. His mate helped him steal a red 1600 Orion GL. Terry kept it in a lock-up garage and, when John rang, he said he would bring down some number plates. During the next few weeks, John contacted Terry and gave the date and time he wanted the car to be delivered to Brookshall Road, Ipswich. Terry was not sure where this was, so John agreed to show him. They drove together in John's car. It was now a silver Peugeot 205 GTi. John explained exactly where the car had to be left and told Terry that he should sit in it and wait until he and the others arrived.

Thursday 25 July, nearly a week before the robbery, John telephoned Terry. He said that the car must be parked in Brookshall Road at 7 p.m. that night. Terry was frightened; he still did not know what the job was.

He immediately went to the lock-up and warmed up the engine. He later drove to where he had been told and, within a couple of minutes, two men arrived – one of them was John. They were wearing suits, shirts and ties. Terry got out of the car and walked away. He did not look back.

Later that evening, John contacted Terry and he was very annoyed. He started swearing because there was hardly any petrol left in the car. He told him to get the car and fill it up immediately. Terry recalls, 'I didn't take the vehicle to a garage, but used two small cans instead. I made several trips, and it cost me about £20.'

Nearly a week later, Wednesday 31 July, John rang Terry again. He said that he was to take the car tomorrow night to Brookshall Road and leave it in exactly the same place as they had discussed. He must be there at 8.30 p.m., and it must be full of petrol. He was aggressive and threatening.

Terry felt sure that the job was going to take place that night. If so, then the target was not going to be a security van as he had thought, but he still had no idea what the plan was.

That Thursday evening, Terry did exactly as he was told. He arrived a few minutes early and, at precisely 8.30 p.m. a silver Peugeot 205 drove past, quite slowly, with three men inside – one of them was John. A few minutes later, John and the dark-haired man walked towards Terry. He got out. This time, as the men drove away, he turned to look and saw the light-haired man who had been at his house before sitting on the back seat. All three men were wearing dark suits, shirts and ties.

Andy Andrews was the manager of Tesco's supermarket in Ipswich. He had been working at the store since it first opened in November 1987.

Andy and his wife, Edna, had been married for twenty years. They lived in a bungalow outside

Colchester town centre and were a close-knit family.

On Thursday 1 August 1991, Andy had taken a day off work. It was a lovely sunny morning and the family decided to go for a picnic, relaxing in the countryside. That evening, Andy had arranged to take Edna out for dinner with some friends. The table was booked for 7.30 p.m. and, afterwards, they returned home, at around 9.30 p.m. James, their youngest son, was watching television and Matthew was still out at a party. It was a hot, sticky evening and Andy went to have a shower.

A little while later, the Andrews family were getting ready for bed. Matthew had still not arrived home from the party, and Andy and Edna were talking in the bedroom. Then the door bell rang.

James called out that he would get it. As he released the latch, the door was pushed open and two men burst in. One had his arms out, grabbing James by the neck, pushing him on to the floor. Andy recalls, 'I could not understand what was happening. I shouted at them to leave James alone. I was pushed against the kitchen door looking straight down the barrels of a shotgun. We were all forced into the lounge and made to sit on the settee. My wife sat in the middle with James and I on the outside. Both men were wearing balaclavas.'

There then followed a series of questions: were they expecting anyone to call round or telephone, were any neighbours likely to drop in, when was Matthew due back? All the time, the family were told to keep their heads down and eyes shut. Edna recalls, 'It just went on from there. I cannot begin to describe the horror.'

When Matthew arrived home, they could hear him parking the car outside; he had taken his mother's Fiat Panda. As the front door opened, Andy, with a shotgun pointing to his head, was told to act normally. He shouted to Matthew to come into the kitchen. Matthew recalls, 'As I walked past the kitchen, Dad called me in, and I just said that I was going to put some things into my room, but he reached out and grabbed my arm. He pulled me into the kitchen and said that there was something he had to tell me. As I walked round the back of him and turned to face him I saw a figure come out of the darkness from the dining room. It startled me. I didn't know what it was at first and then, as it came into the light I saw a man with a shotgun and ammunition belt round his waist. I didn't know what was happening and became very disorientated.'

Matthew was taken into the main bedroom where his mother and brother were lying tied up on the bed. They were very still and he didn't know whether they were hurt or had been drugged. He was very frightened. When the men had tied his ankles and wrists, he was made to lie on the bed next to his mother. He recalls, 'I was told to keep quiet and I just remember Mum leaning across and touching me. She was just letting me know that she was all right.'

Edna herself was extremely frightened. One of the men kept lifting up the corner of her skirt with his gun, taunting her, saying, 'We'll have some fun later.' She recalls, 'I tried to remain calm to reassure the children, but inside my stomach was churning with fear. At one point, I started shaking uncontrollably with fear.'

Andy was told that if he did not cooperate fully, then his wife and children would be killed. He was poked and prodded with the barrels of the gun. Sometimes they opened and closed the guns behind his head. He was terrified. The men explained that they wanted Andy to go to Tesco's and get the takings. In other words, he had to rob his own store. He then had to drive with the money in the boot of his car to a nearby DIY store, leave the car, then walk to the railway station and wait for further instructions. The latest he could leave the car was 3.30 p.m. If he complied, then his family would be released, unharmed.

These instructions were repeated to Andy many times

throughout the night. Eventually he asked if he could write them down to make sure he did not make a mistake. This they agreed to. At some point, another man joined the others. Andy recalls, 'They were using their weapons freely and cockily, often with a sadistic laugh. As it went on, it just seemed to get worse. We were pushed down to a level where we seemed to have no pride left at all, and that really hurt. They made it quite clear that they had killed before and would do so again. They said if I didn't comply then the bodies of my family might never be found.'

The villains helped themselves to booze that was in the house as they carried on making threats and wielding their guns.

Andy was allowed to see his family from time to time, and he was constantly aware of the terrible responsibility he had towards them. After what seemed like a very long time, one of the men said, 'It's five o'clock we'd better get going.' The family were gathered up and taken out of the house. Andy recalled, 'I think my worst moment was after my family had been taken away and I went into the bedroom where they had been held for such a long time. It was terrible. My head ached and I had pains in my chest. I was quite convinced that I had to carry out the plan or my family would be killed. I told myself I had to do it, and the pains I was suffering were a result of stress.'

Andy's family were then forced into the back of Edna's car while two of the men got into the front. All the time, Edna and her sons were told to keep their eyes shut and heads down. They travelled for some time before the car stopped and the men got out. They produced some tape and string and bound the wrists and ankles of Edna and the boys. After a short while, only one man was left with them. He had a knife and gun and was wearing a balaclava.

As day dawned, it began to get very hot. Matthew

recalls, 'The car was camouflaged so nobody could see it, but the windows were kept closed. We were tied up very tightly and the three of us were sitting in the back of a very small car. It really was unbearable and very hot. We had no idea what was happening to Dad, and there were constant threats that we would be killed. The man who stayed with us had a gun and a very long kitchen knife. He sat by the car all day, using it calmly to carve wood, constantly checking on us and threatening us. It was very, very frightening.'

Terry woke up with a start. It was 6.30 a.m. and somebody was banging on the door. He rushed to the bedroom window and looked out. His family were all in bed. John was standing on the doorstep holding a black bag and what appeared to be a couple of pillowcases. Terry let him in and John walked straight past him into the living room, then, as Terry made to shut the door, John shouted, 'Leave it, matey's coming.' A few minutes later, the dark-haired man arrived.

They emptied the pillowcases on to the floor. Suits, shirts, shoes and a dark-coloured wig fell out, along with string and parcel tape. John said to Terry, 'Burn it. Whatever happens everything has got to be burnt.' In another bag was a double-barrelled shotgun and cartridge belt. John said, 'Hide it. I'll collect it in a few days.'

Both men then went upstairs to have a wash. John explained that it was going to be a long day and he wanted to watch some videos to help pass the time. He drove Terry to the garage where they bought petrol, to burn the clothes, and videos.

Shortly afterwards, they returned to the house and the two men fell asleep while Terry went outside to make a bonfire. They woke about 1.30 p.m. had a drink and left. About an hour later, they returned. Neither man explained where they had been, but both seemed to be on edge. John asked Terry to do one more thing for him. He asked him to drive a car. He also handed Terry a piece of paper that had the word 'Samaritans' at the top with a phone number. There followed a list of instructions that referred to a robbery at Tesco's and the fact that the family had been abducted.

Terry recalls, 'This was the first time that I had really known what was happening and I refused to do it. I said I didn't want anything more to do with what was happening. John was very firm and said I had to do it. I felt very intimidated and didn't see that I had much alternative.'

Andy Andrews drove into work that morning, and tried to act as though everything was normal. He recalls, 'The time dragged on. I tried to do some paperwork, but couldn't concentrate. I was very worried. During my lunch hour I decided that I would have to confide in a few of my staff. I just couldn't walk out carrying all the money and, even if I did, then it was quite possible someone would raise the alarm after I'd gone. I had to give the villains an hour after I'd dropped off the cash and, if the alarm was raised, I could lose my family. I pleaded with my staff to help me. I found it very hard, but I explained what had happened. I told them that as soon as my family were safe, I was going to ring 999, and that if they hadn't heard from the police by 5 p.m. then they should raise the alarm.'

Andy got into his red Rover and left the store at 3.05 p.m. He had with him a security guard because it crossed his mind that the police might not believe him. He drove as instructed to the DIY store and parked the car. He left the money in the boot and made his way to the railway station.

It was a very hot day, and Andy's family had no idea how long they were going to be kept cramped together in the back of the car. On several occasions, Edna and the boys asked for the window to be opened. Edna remembers, 'I was convinced they would kill us because we had seen their faces during the night. We weren't allowed to move – if we did, the man guarding us would poke his gun at us and threaten to kill us. The heat was unbearable and all the time the fear was with us.'

Then, from nowhere, a car horn suddenly started beeping. It sounded several times in rapid succession. It was about 3.20 p.m. The family looked up and saw their guard run down a path towards the noise of the car. They could not see anything, but the man disappeared.

After a few minutes, when Edna and the boys thought they were safe, they managed to untie their arms and legs and get out of the car. They walked to the main road, and came across a builder's yard. Edna said to the receptionist, 'Please can you help us, can we make a phone call, we've just managed to release ourselves.' Edna explained to the police what had happened.

Terry got out of John's car and made his way towards a car in a DIY car park on the outskirts of Ipswich, which John had pointed out. It was the red Rover. He started the ignition, but found that it was an automatic. He'd never driven an automatic before and found himself kangarooing through the car park. When he got on to the main road, he was still having difficulty with the controls, then he looked in his mirror and saw John behind him in the silver Peugeot. He was waving his arm out of the window, telling him to go faster. Gradually, as he became more familiar with the controls, Terry speeded up and John took the lead and they carried on for about eighteen miles before he stopped in Sainsbury's car park, Colchester.

They got out and John went round to the boot of the Rover and asked Terry to open it. John said, 'Gloves off. Take your gloves off,' but Terry refused. He realized that John wanted him to leave his fingerprints behind. When the Peugeot was loaded with the takings, John immediately drove off. Terry got a taxi into Colchester town centre, and then a train back to Ipswich. He never saw John again.

Andy Andrews waited at the railway station for nearly an hour. Nobody turned up and he was very worried, so he rang the police: 'The deadline had passed and I thought something had gone wrong, so I dialled 999. They told me my wife and family were safe. I remember dropping the phone and sort of trying to find somewhere to hide. I was just so tearful, I couldn't control myself. Not a soul came near me, they must have thought I was a bit weird and strange. I just howled. I was so relieved that they were safe.'

Detective Superintendent Malcolm Hargreaves was tidying up and about to go off duty for the weekend when the phone call came through late on Friday afternoon. Although based at Essex Police Headquarters in Chelmsford, he was the senior officer in charge of the north of the county. He was therefore immediately put in charge of the investigation, and arranged for an incident room to be set up in Colchester. His first reaction was relief that the Andrews family, although traumatized, were now safe.

Detective Superintendent Malcolm Hargreaves is a family man. He had served the police force for thirty years and is well-respected by his colleagues.

Detective Inspector Dick Block was acting as Chief Inspector at Colchester while his colleague was away, so he automatically became the second in command, and Detective Sergeant Graeme Bull, who was on duty, became his deputy.

Once the call was received everyone moved quickly. Detective Inspector Block went to the Andrews family home while Detective Sergeant Bull coordinated the operation from base. Telephone calls were coming in thick and fast, and nobody could quite believe that such a serious inquiry was beginning late on a Friday afternoon.

On hearing the details of the robbery, Detective

Inspector Block was particularly concerned for the family and anxious to make sure that they were as comfortable as possible. Arrangements were made for them to be brought back to Colchester and, because of the trauma they had suffered, it was decided not to take any statements from them until the following day. That night, the family stayed in a hotel, and a liaison officer was appointed to work with them.

A forensic team was sent to their home and the house was sealed off. It was treated as if it had been a murder scene, and officers spent nearly two days scouring the place for clues.

That evening, at around 11 p.m., the police held a briefing. Only the bare bones of the story were known at this time, but, on hearing the details, a police officer said that two weeks earlier she had heard from an informant that Tesco's was going to be the subject of some criminal activity and that the people involved were Terry Allen and Jack Marsh. The police had been watching the supermarket from time to time, but had come up with nothing.

The next morning, when Terry saw all the newspaper reports, he decided to get rid of the gun and cartridges that John had left behind. He hid them in a bin liner among some clothing and asked a neighbour to look after them for him. On Sunday, John rang and said that he would be sending him £2000 for his part in the robbery. The next day, the dark-haired man rang and said he would be sending the money soon, and that, in the meantime, he should keep a low profile, then everything would be fine. However, unbeknown to any of the robbers, Terry was secretly boasting to friends about his part in the robbery: 'They degraded me and made me feel a real joey. I was getting no thanks. I just felt that they were trespassing on my property. I was doing everything for them. So, a couple of days after the job, I boasted that I was there. I wanted people to look at me as if I was Mr Big. I pretended that I had a lot more to do with it than I really had.' This was to be his biggest mistake.

The police immediately latched on to the two names Terry Allen and Jack Marsh and, the next morning, Detective Inspector Dick Block and Detective Sergeant Graeme Bull were despatched to find out more about them (these two officers ran the day-to-day aspects of the inquiry).

The robbery made headline news, and it quickly became known that there was a £30 000 reward on offer. Detective Inspector Block recalls, 'Once word was out about the large amount of money on offer, informants began to crawl out of the woodwork. The information was coming in thick and fast. The word on the street was that the team were from London, but two local men had helped to set it up. They were Terry Allen and Jack Marsh.'

One informant provided even *better* news for the police. He met detectives in a pub and told them that not only was Terry Allen involved in the job, but that he had items used in the job stashed away at his house, and was expecting a parcel any day that would contain his share of the money.

This was fantastic news for the police. If they could catch him receiving the money, then they would be able to arrest him immediately. They knew from enquiries that they had made, and from the descriptions of the offenders given by the Andrews family, that Terry Allen and Jack Marsh were not the robbers, but they did believe that they could lead them straight to the men responsible.

Some police officers camped out in the Ipswich sorting office, waiting for the parcel of money to arrive. They were anxious to recover it as quickly as possible because they had no idea what else might have been inside with the money – fingerprints, perhaps a letter, an address, anything at all. They had been granted a warrant from the Home Secretary authorizing them to do this, but, when the package arrived, the Post Office insisted that the mail had to be delivered in the normal way. This, of course, caused problems, but the police got round it, first, by keeping the postman due to deliver the package under surveillance to make sure it did not disappear *en route*, and, second, a police officer dressed in a postman's uniform waited near Terry's house with a fake parcel and, just before the real package was delivered, he knocked on the door. Terry came downstairs and, while he was signing for it, the police pounced on him.

When the real postman came round the corner, he saw a swarm of officers and handed the package over to a police officer, who signed for it. The police wanted to make sure that Terry Allen never touched the package because it had to go as quickly as possible to forensic experts to be searched for clues. It would have been quite easy for vital evidence to have been destroyed.

The police, then, immediately arrested Terry Allen and put him in the back of the van before he really knew what had happened. Terry recalls, 'I was seconds away from getting a package with loads of money in it. I'd never even seen £200 let alone £2000. I was over the moon. I was skint and now I felt really happy. Then, before I had time to look at it, I was cuffed and sitting in the back of the van. I was thinking, Jesus Christ, what am I going to do? What am I going to say to them? I knew I was going to be in for a hard time because of the seriousness of the crime, and it was really a question of how much they knew. In the end, it turned out that they knew far more than me.'

Terry Allen was interviewed by Detective Inspector Dick Block and Detective Sergeant Graeme Bull. At this stage in the inquiry, the police were very optimistic. They had arrested a number of people, including Jack

Marsh, and had recovered a gun, and now they had the package containing the money.

The Andrews family spent a considerable amount of time going meticulously over the night's events, trying to be as accurate as possible. They were interviewed in a special sympathy suite and the interviewing officer remembers that Edna was 'the worst trauma victim she had ever come across', such was the effect these terrible men had had on their lives.

The family had received only one glass of water between them during their eighteen-hour ordeal, and this was only because Edna had requested it. No food or other beverages had been offered.

Interviewing each member of the family and piecing all the information together was a very long process. The family were very frightened of any repercussions and, understandably, took a long time before giving detailed descriptions of the offenders.

Meanwhile, Jack Marsh had been interviewed by Detective Sergeant Bull and he had tried to arrange some kind of deal with the police for information. Sergeant Bull recalls, 'Jack was a wily old bird who was, without doubt, looking after his own interests. He was trying to give us sufficient to placate us and lessen the damage against him.' Jack did admit to introducing the German to Terry Allen, but he gave little away and, at the end of the inquiry, the police were still uncertain as to how much he really knew.

It was not until they spoke to Terry Allen that more details began to emerge. Detective Inspector Dick Block began by asking Terry for the names of the robbers. Terry replied:

'I don't know, honest. Jack Marsh introduced me to this German bloke called John. He said he wanted to do a bit of business.'
'What do you know about Jack Marsh?'

'I've known him for quite a while. He used to come round a lot since his wife died. I sort of looked up to him.'

'So, Jack introduced you to the German. When did you see him again?'

'I saw him a lot after that. He'd ring me up and tell me he'd be coming down. I'd send my wife and kids out. I didn't want them involved. He scared me.'

Initially, the police found it difficult to understand exactly what Terry Allen knew because of his reluctance to talk. He was frightened of the seriousness of the crime in which he had become embroiled. He was worried that the gang might attack him and his family or seek retribution in some other way. In the beginning, he was not very helpful.

The police found it incredible that Terry had met the robbers on many occasions over a six-month period, helped them plan a major armed robbery, yet did not know any of their names. Detective Inspector Block recalls, 'Initially he was reluctant to tell us his part in the offences and even more reluctant, I felt, to tell us who the people were that were really responsible, and it took a long time for him to convince me that he didn't actually know their names, but the longer I interviewed him, the more convinced I became. It was just a matter of listening to him and watching him. He seemed to try so hard. You could see him straining to tell me things, even the simplest of things that he thought would help, like how many sugars the men had in their tea and coffee. He told me about some toys the German had given to his kids, and batteries he had put in to make them work, which only he could have touched, and we would therefore be able to get his fingerprints.'

At this point in the investigation, several of the officers were divided about Terry Allen and the information he had given. Detective Superintendent Malcolm

Hargreaves recalls, 'We had to keep an open mind, but I and a number of other officers found it hard to believe that he didn't know more than he was saying. It's difficult to believe that a man could have been involved in planning a job like this for some months and yet he, allegedly, didn't know the name of the man, the ringleader, his phone number or his address. Although I had reservations, that's not an unhealthy thing to have. You need a balance across the team, everyone questioning different aspects of the inquiry.'

Despite not knowing their names, Terry Allen was now giving lots of details about the other members of the team – cars they drove, habits they had – and it seemed that the more he told them, the more convinced officers were that he must be telling the truth.

Terry was asked to put together Photofits of the offenders. He sat with a policewoman for nearly two hours, picking out the same 'eyes' over and over again. The policewoman recalls, 'I got the impression that he was just messing me about. I didn't believe anything that he was doing. He was definitely doing a portrait of someone, whether it be his uncle or someone, I don't know, but I didn't think he was doing a Photofit of our robbers.' In fact, the Photofits turned out to be very accurate and, when a photograph of the real German came into the office, only then did she realize that Terry had actually been trying his best.

While Detective Inspector Block and Detective Sergeant Bull were carrying on with the interview, Detective Superintendent Hargreaves and the team were making enquiries all over the country to see whether any more offences could be linked with this particular gang. Three other jobs came to light and officers were immediately despatched to check them out. One was a robbery in Kelvedon of Barclays Bank where the family was held hostage in similar circumstances. Detective Superintendent Hargreaves recalls, 'After a couple of weeks, I was absolutely convinced that the Kelvedon job was linked to ours. It's only about ten miles from Colchester and there were a number of striking similarities.'

The Kelvedon raid in April 1989 had actually been featured on *Crimewatch* but, despite a good response, nobody had been charged with the offence. After several meetings, detectives decided to contact *Crimewatch* again. They had so much detail about the German – down to the kind of cigarettes he smoked – that they felt confident someone must recognize the Photofit.

When the investigating team rang the *Crimewatch* production office, it was decided to produce a filmed reconstruction. However, because the villains had specifically threatened the family regarding going on the programme, the police provided them with twenty-four-hour protection.

This was a particularly difficult reconstruction for *Crimewatch* to do because the crime itself was so frightening. It had taken place in the family home, the victims had been tormented with guns and had been kidnapped for many hours before the villains had finally got what they wanted. However, because there were so many clues – the Photofit of the German, the two cars he had been known to drive, and a lot of personal detail about the men themselves – everyone felt sure of a success. Somebody must know something, and it was decided to concentrate on these points of appeal, and show little of what actually happened in the Andrews house.

The descriptions of the attackers were the strongest clues we had and so it was important to find good look-a-like actors for the reconstruction. This is a difficult element of the programme and, even though *Crimewatch* is a monthly programme, the schedule leading up to transmission is quite tight. Once the reconstruction cases have been chosen, the team has only a few days to organize everything before filming begins. In the space of about three days, the actors have to be auditioned, the research has to be finalized and the script complete. Unfortunately, only one day is allocated for all auditions and the choice, therefore, is limited. Researchers have been known to spend the entire day and night searching for the right face. Frequently, time is so short that the director has to audition in the town where the film is being made and, very often, it can be the night before filming. *Crimewatch* also relies a great deal on the goodwill of the general public. As in this particular case where a silver Peugeot and four-wheel drive vehicle were required, garage owners and other individuals frequently lend their vehicles to the programme for the duration of the filming.

The reconstruction was broadcast on 10 October 1991 and the response was overwhelming. Detective Superintendent Hargreaves recalls, '*Crimewatch* was a fantastic night. We had over 300 calls to the studio alone, and it was impossible for us to go through all of them immediately to analyse what we'd got, but we felt confident that in those calls somewhere were the ones that would give us the name of "the German", as we called him.'

Two days after the *Crimewatch* programme, the police had checked and analysed all the information. In particular, there were three calls that gave the same address for the German. One of these came from a car dealer who said he had recently sold a four-wheel drive vehicle to a German fitting the description, and the buyer had paid with notes taken out of a plastic bag. Other callers gave specific details about the German and a policewoman had some interesting information. She had been working on Thursday night so her husband video taped *Crimewatch* and she watched it the following morning while having her breakfast. When she saw the Photofit of the German, she instantly recognized him.

The previous evening, she had been doing routine vehicle checks along Vauxhall Bridge Road, south

London, when a man driving a four-wheel drive vehicle pulled away very quickly from the traffic lights. She stopped him and asked to see his documents. He had a strong accent and said he was German. The address on his licence was Aldershot, and he explained that, although that was where he lived, he was visiting his girlfriend in London. The policewoman recalls, 'He was very narked when I pulled him over and a bit aggressive. I told him not to take that attitude with me and eventually he calmed down a bit. He had the presence of a body builder, someone who could handle themselves. There were other police officers in the area and that's probably why he calmed down. His eyes were very striking. They stood out and he stared at me the whole time, he never looked away. All his documents were in order so I let him go.'

The name the police were given was Karl Schultz. A couple of informants had given this same Aldershot address and so a surveillance team was immediately despatched to watch the premises. Detective Superintendent Hargreaves recalls, 'We were hoping that the German was still there, or still in the vicinity, and that we might see him coming or going from the house, but, in fact, we didn't see anything at all and I decided we couldn't wait any longer.' So, three days after *Crimewatch*, the police decided to mount an armed raid on the premises.

When officers raided the house, the only person there was a young woman. She was Karl Schultz's girlfriend and said she had not seen him for a couple of days. She was taken to the police station for questioning. She explained that Karl Schultz had said that he needed to get away for a while, but she had no idea where he had gone or for how long. She had no contact address for him – all his numbers were in a black book that he always kept on him. They had been together for five years, but it seemed that she knew little about him.

Detective Sergeant Graeme Bull remembers, 'She was very suspicious of us initially and didn't want to believe what we were telling her. In the end, she was a victim herself. She was totally taken in by him, believed him, trusted him, and, of course, her life was shattered when the truth finally came out.'

Karl Schultz's girlfriend did, however, tell the police that he was keen on mountaineering and frequently went climbing in Wales. He had told her he was an engineer, born in Germany. She also gave the police a detailed description of the four-wheel drive vehicle he was driving, saying he had sold his previous one only a week ago.

Detective Superintendent Hargreaves recalls, 'We had a hunch that he really had gone to Wales. Details given to us by his girlfriend seemed to suggest this, so I had a telex message sent to the mid Wales and North Wales police forces, asking them to search for his current vehicle. It stated that the driver was armed and very dangerous.'

Later that night, a police patrol car was driving through Capel Curig, North Wales, when the police officers in it saw what they thought was Karl Schultz's vehicle parked in the car park of the Cobden Arms Hotel. They immediately contacted officers at Betws-y-Coed, where a special incident room had been set up.

Three officers were sent to the hotel to check the vehicle, make sure it was the one they were looking for, and to confirm that Karl Schultz was still driving it. Their brief was to take a look around and try to find Karl Schultz. If he was on the premises, they had to speak to the licensee and find out how long he was staying. Once they had the information, they were to feed it back to the incident room. As he was known to be a dangerous, armed criminal, the plan was not to approach him as yet.

However, as soon as the police officers walked into

the hotel's lobby, they saw a man walking towards them. He had come from the direction of the toilets and he looked exactly like the Photofit. They felt sure it was the German. He went into the lounge bar, so they followed him.

The detectives ordered a drink. From the bar, they could monitor his movements. He was sitting with a woman at a table by the window, and they presumed she was his girlfriend. Unfortunately, the licensee and a member of his family were drinking on the same side of the bar as the customers, and they were in close proximity to Karl Schultz. As a result, the officers dared not approach him in case they blew their cover.

After some time, Karl Schultz got up with the woman and made to leave the hotel. One of the officers went and phoned the incident room to tell them what was happening. A surveillance unit was put on alert to follow him if he left the building, and the firearms team were put on standby. The plan was not to arrest him inside the hotel because of the danger of a possible hostage situation.

Karl Schultz and his girlfriend went out of the entrance to the hotel, towards a waiting car, a taxi. After they had left, one of the officers noticed that the woman had left her handbag behind. He told the licensee, who quickly ran out with it. When he came back, the officers made themselves known and started asking questions about Karl Schultz. While they were talking, they realized that Karl Schultz was just seeing the woman off, and he was now making his way back towards the hotel.

They did not have time to finish their conversation before Karl Schultz walked into the bar. One of them recalled, 'I was concerned at this point that the licensee might inadvertently tell Schultz that we had been making enquiries about him and I was concerned that the situation might develop into a hostage' situation, or that Schultz might try to escape.'

When Karl Schultz walked back in, he went towards the officers who were standing at the bar and the licensee shouted, 'These are the gentlemen who saw the handbag.' Karl Schultz thanked them and turned to face the bar. The policemen decided they had to act quickly before the situation got out of control. An officer stood either side of Karl Schultz and they pulled him to the ground and handcuffed him. One of the officers recalls, 'We were fortunate that we had surprise on our side to enable us to overpower this violent man. The plan was not to attempt to take him, unarmed and with just the three of us, but the element of surprise enabled us to do so.'

When Karl Schultz was told that he was under arrest, he made one comment, 'You have been watching too much television.'

Back in Essex, Detective Superintendent Hargreaves and his team were waiting by the telephone. Detective Sergeant Bull and another officer had already set off for Wales to help look for Karl Schultz, and he was delighted when he received a call saying that the four-wheel drive vehicle had been found: 'I was pleased to know that we were on the right track. Having said that, I was gutted that I wasn't going to be there when they found him. We'd all worked so hard on the case, and I wanted to see his reaction. I drove pretty quickly, but when I got to the hotel, they'd arrested him ten minutes earlier.'

It had been a tense night for everyone. Detective Superintendent Hargreaves remembers, 'I was in the incident room burning the midnight oil and smoking a lot of cigarettes and drinking hundreds of cups of coffee. Although the vehicle had been spotted on the hotel forecourt, there was always the fear that, for one reason or another, we'd miss him, and I was worried that if we missed him, then he would do a runner, perhaps to Europe, and then we would really have been in difficulty. Then the call came through, and we just shouted aloud, releasing all our nervous energy. The North Wales police had done a tremendous job.'

The police searched Karl Schultz's room and found his black book. This, together with all his belongings, were taken back to Essex. Karl Schultz also had to be taken back to Essex in a police car. It was a very long journey and officers were frightened that he might make some attempt to escape. They drove as quickly as possible. One officer sat close to him in the back, so he was in a position to feel any slight movement, and another officer sat in the front, looking at him in the mirror on the visor at all times. It was a very quiet, strenuous journey, with no stops and no major conversation, apart from the occasional offering of cigarettes and sweets.

Detective Sergeant Bull had faxed pages from Karl Schultz's address book to the incident room in Colchester. It was all in code and needed to be looked at immediately. Everyone's mind was now centred on catching the other two robbers. The police felt sure that Karl Schultz's book would hold the vital clue.

It only took a few hours to crack the code, and the police then had before them several names and numbers. They were particularly interested in an address in Southend because Terry Allen had mentioned Southend in his interviews. He could give no specific details, but the police felt sure it might have some connection with the other robbers.

Meanwhile, fingerprints were taken from Karl Schultz and, when Detective Sergeant Bull who was going to interview him, asked, 'What do you think these will tell us?' Karl Schultz, with a smirk on his face, replied, 'That's for you to find out.' Throughout the preliminaries, when Karl Schultz was asked any questions, he replied, 'No comment.' Detective Sergeant Bull remembers, 'I thought initially that he was making no comment because he didn't want to incriminate himself, but then I realized that he was treating it more as a game than any-thing else. I think he's very, very deep and he's obviously got very strong willpower. He constantly looked at me and smiled, trying to intimidate me.'

At the same time, officers, through Karl Schultz's address book, had come across the two names Robert Moore and Sean Wain. These were checked with the records department and, when detectives looked at their photographs, they were identical to the Photofit pictures made with the help of Terry Allen. Police also discovered that they owned a silver Peugeot and an XR2. It all began to fall into place.

They also had an address, so officers were sent with a firearms team, to check if they were there. Neither man was at his home. Apparently they were working together in a place not far from Southend, about twenty miles away. Officers arrived in the early hours of the morning, only to discover that the men were not there either and that the only person in the house was a woman. She had no idea where they were.

Officers searched the premises, and then rang Detective Superintendent Hargreaves with the bad news. He was adamant: 'Don't tell me this! You can stay out on the road, and don't come back without them.'

It was thought that the men would still be driving the silver Peugeot, so officers decided to split up and search the area. After a short time, it was spotted parked next to a telephone box. The two men were just getting back into it. All officers were immediately called to the area and they followed until they could find a suitable place to make an arrest. It was essential that this happened away from other drivers and pedestrians because they were very dangerous men and likely to be armed.

The silver Peugeot approached a T junction on a quiet section of road. Looking around, the detectives thought this was the opportunity they had been waiting for. The word was given and, within seconds, four cars had surrounded the Peugeot, blocking the road. Before the two suspects knew what was happening, they had been pulled out of the car and handcuffed. Neither of them spoke.

Throughout the investigation, the Andrews family was in constant touch with the police and, when the men were arrested, particularly the German, Andy was relieved. He recalled, 'The fact that he was in custody was a great relief. We knew that there were other people involved, but he was the ringleader. My wife wasn't at all relieved. She said that she felt much *worse* because she knew he was a very devious person; she thought he would somehow convince them that he wasn't involved, and then he would come back for us.'

Back at Colchester, the police had uncovered some extraordinary information about Karl Schultz. They discovered that, far from being the German he claimed to be, he was, in fact, John Calton from Sheffield, who had previously had a Yorkshire accent. He was one of seven children and had not seen his mother for over twenty years. He had been in prison before for a series of robberies of building societies. However, when confronted with these details, John Calton always replied, 'No comment' and, even though his cover was now blown, he never went back to speaking with his native Yorkshire accent.

The police again interviewed his girlfriend in London and it transpired that, although they had been together for five years, he had never revealed his true identity. She truly believed he was German.

As for his girlfriend in Wales, she had only known him for a few months and was amazed when he was arrested. She, too, believed that he was German. He had told her that he was an only child, had gone to boarding school and was now an engineer. He acted like he was proud to be German, and he even called his dog 'Bismarck'. She recalls, 'He acted just the opposite to what he was really like. He used to buy me flowers or chocolates, and he was very kind, considerate and funny. He went out of his way to make me feel special – sometimes I would have four letters a day from him. He could charm the birds out of the trees, and I didn't think he had a bad bone in his body. He even stopped to feed the squirrels. I was amazed and disgusted when I found out the truth about him. It just goes to show how wrong you can be about someone and I just hope he's really miserable because of all the suffering he has caused to other people. I hope they keep him locked up for a very long time.'

Once Sean Wain and Robert Moore had been arrested, they were brought to the station to be interviewed. Both men refused to answer any questions.

Detective Superintendent Hargreaves and his team were now in the process of gathering together as much evidence as possible before they brought charges. They had a lot of circumstantial evidence:

- the car dealer had said that a man with a German accent calling himself Karl Schultz had paid cash for several vehicles, each purchase being made just days after the offence had been committed

- once the police had visited Karl Schultz's address, his girlfriend's description fitted with what Terry Allen had said in that she said he liked mountaineering, was German, had a strong accent, and kept all his contact numbers in a black book

- Karl Schultz's fingerprints and those of Sean Wain and Robert Moore were found at Terry Allen's house

- witnesses had come forward saying that they had seen three men dressed in suits in a red Orion, again corroborating everything Terry had said

- the police found a gun in Karl Schultz's garage with Sean Wain's fingerprints on it.

Despite all of this, the police had not one hard piece of evidence that put either of the three men inside the family home or at Tesco's. When they searched the home, they found no forensic evidence – no fingerprints, nothing. What was crucial now was to hold an identification parade with the Andrews family and the family taken hostage during the Kelvedon robbery to see if they could identify their assailants. If they could, then, together with all the circumstantial evidence, the police felt they were home and dry.

Detective Superintendent Hargreaves recalls what it was like on the day of the identification parade for the investigating team: 'We waited in an ante-room whilst the witnesses filed past the men. We could see from a monitor everything that was going on. The atmosphere was really tense – it was the culmination of all we had been working towards, and none of us could be sure of the outcome.'

Edna Andrews was one of the first to walk along the line. She immediately picked out John Calton, and there were screams of delight from the ante-room, where the investigation team were watching and waiting. In fact, both John Calton and Robert Moore were identified by some members of the Andrews family. John Calton was not only picked out by the Andrews family, but by the Kelvedon family as well.

Detective Superintendent Hargreaves and his team were delighted. The final piece of the jigsaw was now in place: 'It was an amazing investigation. The most satisfying inquiry that I've ever worked on. The amount of teamwork that went into it and the result that we got was very satisfying, not just for us, but for the victims who went through absolutely horrific ordeals.'

The case was heard at Chelmsford Crown Court during October and November 1992.

Terry Allen gave evidence against his co-accused and, before sentencing him, the judge said, 'I will bear in mind the assistance you gave at very considerable risk to yourself and very probably your family. You have given very considerable help in the administration of justice by having the courage to give evidence in court. I intend to make a very dramatic reduction in the sentence.' Terry Allen was sentenced to three years' imprisonment.

The judge, when sentencing the accused, said this: 'Claton, Moore and Wain, it is rare, fortunately, I find that I have men in front of me who are not only wicked as you are, but it is rare that I find people in front of me who are also evil. The way that you carried out these brutal and cruel robberies (and the money in one sense pales into insignificance) and the kidnap, because that is what it comes to, of honest, ordinary, decent people and the vile cruelty which you showed, showed no mercy; and you can expect little from me. If ever there was a case where I am dealing with men who are dangerous and from whom the public need a long period of protection, it is you three.'

John Calton was sentenced to twenty-five years' imprisonment.

As for Sean Wain and Robert Moore, the judge said, 'As far as you are concerned, evil and wicked though you are, you were not the ringleaders. You will go both of you ... to prison for twenty years.'

Jack Marsh was sentenced to one year's imprisonment.

For the police, it was a tremendous result; the three main culprits received a total of sixty-five years' imprisonment. The job is now over for them, but, unfortunately, such was the terror imposed on the Andrews family that night, that their fear lives on. Andy recalls, 'There's still things that happen to us late at night, in the middle of the night or during the day. Things that remind us about what's gone on. We're reassured that this will subside with time, but it's been three years now, and there are still things that give me a start – a smell, a

231

noise, a sound – and it brings a shiver down my spine. I wish it wasn't there. I wish we could turn the clock back and we could have avoided the situation. These people have affected our lives forever. It might diminish, but it will never go away.'

John Calton has never resumed his true identity. He retained his German accent throughout the trial, and has continued to use it while serving his prison sentence.